REVERSE MARKETING

The New Buyer–Supplier Relationship

Michiel R. Leenders

David L. Blenkhorn

THE FREE PRESS
A Division of Macmillan, Inc.
NEW YORK

Maxwell Macmillan Canada
TORONTO

Maxwell Macmillan International
NEW YORK   OXFORD   SINGAPORE   SYDNEY

The Free Press
A Division of Macmillan, Inc.
866 Third Avenue, New York, N.Y. 10022

Maxwell Macmillan Canada, Inc.
1200 Eglinton Avenue East
Suite 200
Don Mills, Ontario M3C 3N1

Macmillan, Inc. is part of the Maxwell Communication
Group of Companies.

Printed in the United States of America

printing number

4 5 6 7 8 9 10

Library of Congress Cataloging-in-Publication Data

Leenders, Michiel R.
Reverse marketing.

1. Industrial procurement.   I. Blenkhorn, David L.
II. Title.
HD39.5.L435   1988   658.7'2   87–15146
ISBN 0-02-918381-2

Contents

Preface

THIS book was written because the authors strongly believe that the supply function can make a significant contribution to organizational objectives and strategy. Reverse marketing offers an exciting, proactive, imaginative opportunity to broaden supply's traditional perspective.

Research on this topic was started by Michiel R. Leenders for his doctoral thesis at the Graduate School of Business Administration at Harvard University over twenty years ago. He has continued to work in this area since that time and was joined by David L. Blenkhorn in 1980. As a team they undertook the task of researching reverse marketing on a world-wide basis and of documenting the accomplishments of private and public organizations.

The purpose is to define reverse marketing both by theory and practice and to show how and why it should be carried out. Reverse marketing holds out a challenge to the practitioner to set seemingly impossible targets and achieve them. It requires a long-term, strategic perspective congruent with the organization's objectives and strategies. The authors are now more convinced than ever that reverse marketing is synonymous with a top management perspective on supply potential.

This book examines the reverse marketing concept in its widest context. Extensive research has been undertaken to document successful and unsuccessful reverse marketing efforts. Each chapter will contain at least one extensive description of a reverse marketing attempt, complemented by a variety of smaller examples for contrast and comparison. The organization of this text is as follows: The first chapter presents an overview of reverse marketing; the second identifies the reverse marketing framework. The third will address value and price; the fourth, technology; the fifth, social and political concerns; the sixth, a variety of topics including the Japanese experience, global companies, and just-in-time efforts; and the seventh, supplier size. The final chapter will summarize and provide conclusions.

Acknowledgments

THE authors acknowledge with deep thanks the contributions of all of the practitioners who showed the way by their reverse marketing efforts. For a variety of reasons, including modesty, many requested anonymity. Therefore, the names of most companies and individuals have been disguised in the text.

This book and the research for it received the support of many different people. We would like to thank our respective deans, Dean Charles B. Johnston of the School of Business Administration of the University of Western Ontario and Dean J. Alex Murray of the School of Business and Economics, Wilfrid Laurier University, for the institutional support we received. The Western Ontario District of the Purchasing Management Association of Canada and the Department of External Affairs of the Government of Canada (Industry, Trade and Commerce) generously provided research grants to cover various expenses including travel. Secretarial assistance came from Loretta Peregrina and from Elsie Grogan, who was responsible for the final manuscript.

We also appreciate the support of our friends, colleagues, and family members. A book is always easier to start than to finish and warm support helps smooth the way.

To translate academic language into managerial sense is not an easy task, and we are very much in debt to the editorial staff of The Free Press, notably, Bob Wallace, Karen Ott, and Celia Knight, for their guidance and suggestions.

CHAPTER 1

Reverse Marketing

Two executives walk briskly into a supplier's head office. Their mission: to persuade the vendor's managers to accept a proposal that makes a lot of sense for both organizations, yet represents a substantial departure from the vendor's normal way of doing business. The activity: reverse marketing. The two executives representing the buying organization, its president and vice president of materials, both know that without their initiative the vendor is unlikely to volunteer what their organization needs.

Unusual behavior? Neither the involvement of the president nor the aggressive pursuit of a potential supplier are unusual for the managers whose reverse marketing efforts are documented in this book. Why? Because they believe that the effective management of supply is a key factor in the achievement of organizational objectives. And they also recognize the potential inherent in imaginative and aggressive management of the supply function. They recognize that with the pressures of global competition, economic, political, and social change and uncertainties, the need for continuing improvement, renewed emphasis on quality, the introduction of just-in-time systems, and world-class manufacturing, it is no longer good enough to wait for suppliers to carry the ball.

In his fascinating book, *Marketing High Technology,*[1] William H. Davidow says:

> It has always been incredible to me how insensitive companies can be to their customers. Most of them don't seem to understand that their future business depends on having the same customer come back again and again.

1

He also says:

> Most marketing people have very high energy levels. They are very good at explaining why anything they do is effective. When management looks at marketing, it is easy for it to come away dazzled by a slick presentation. After all, if marketing people can sell products, they ought to be able to sell their most important product, themselves.[2]

And to justify the building of the organization around the marketing core, Davidow also notes:

> Companies exist to satisfy the customer. It is a rare organization that will do so without a constant push from marketing. *If the marketing group is not the driving organization to look after customer interests, who will?* [Italics ours.][3]

The obvious answer:

THE CUSTOMER!

Reverse marketing is an aggressive and imaginative approach to achieving supply objectives. The purchaser takes the initiative in making the proposal. The goal is to satisfy both short- and long-term supply objectives.

This book will not only substantiate reverse marketing's potential, but also provide information on the why, what, who, how, where, and when. It is hoped that by showing how outstanding results can be accomplished practitioners will be encouraged to give reverse marketing an honest try.

Reverse marketing requires close work with an existing or a new vendor to meet ambitious supply objectives. This may involve persuading a reluctant vendor to become a supplier; persuading managers inside the purchaser's organization to make what was formerly purchased, or vice versa; persuading users to try a new product, service, or system while persuading a vendor to do likewise; and a host of other tasks. The key is in the two words "initiative" and "persuasion."

The rewards are many. Savings in the 5 to 30 percent range are not uncommon. Reverse marketing permits procurement to contribute effectively to the organization's objectives and strategy. Successful reverse marketing requires cooperation from all levels and most functions in the organization; hence, it enhances the role of the supply function. Reverse marketing is future oriented and requires careful planning and research. It may permit the achievement of seemingly impossible objectives in terms of quality, quantity, price, delivery, and service.

Reverse marketing is more than just a technique or tool. It represents a different perspective on the role of supply and how it should be managed so as to contribute effectively to organizational goals and strategies.

THE SUPPLY FUNCTION

Before reverse marketing is examined in more detail, the supply function itself should be reviewed. No organization is totally self-sufficient. Every organization depends on suppliers to meet a variety of needs in the form of materials, goods, or services.

If one considers any organization simply as an input-output transformation system as in Figure 1–1, it is not difficult to appreciate that the management of the input side is highly relevant to the success of the total system. An easy parallel exists for the human body. Our inputs are what we eat, drink, breathe, see, feel, and hear. We spend a lot of time ensuring that these inputs fit our needs.

The supply function in an organization can contribute substantially to organizational objectives and strategy if it is well organized and managed. How to make sure this function contributes effectively is a challenge to supply managers as well as to the top manager in any public or private organization.

Realization that specialized expertise and top management at-

FIGURE 1–1.
An Organization as an Input-Output Transformation System

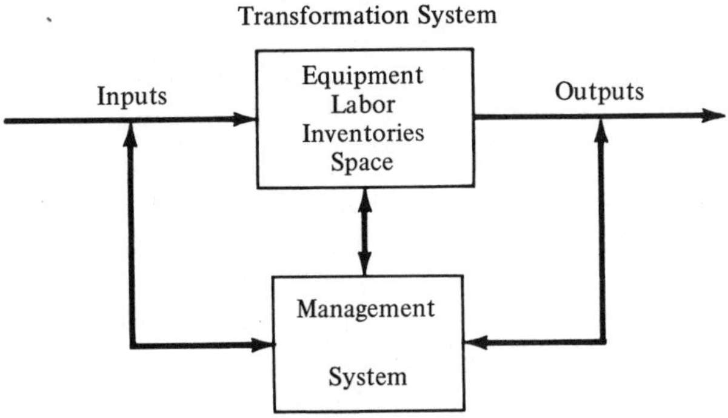

tention may be necessary to obtain most benefits from the supply function has been slower in coming than might at first be expected. For example, the marketing area, which represents the mirror image to the supply function, has enjoyed substantial management and academic interest for a longer period, as has accounting. The two world wars, difficult economic times, shortages and overages of critical materials have served as reminders that inattention to the supply area can be extremely costly to an organization. Unfortunately, these learning periods have reinforced the negative, rather than the positive side of supply. Obviously, neglect in input management, as in any other management area, will result in painful experiences. But it is not simply the avoidance of pain that calls for management attention in supply. It is the attainment of opportunities not yet claimed that represents the exciting potential of supply.

The communication lines of supply reach into every part of every organization, even if requirements are as simple as pens and paper. Ensuring that all the needs of the whole organization are met in terms of quality, quantity, delivery, cost, service, and continuity has traditionally required a tremendous amount of time and effort. Almost invariably, changes in plans and problems in the market create last minute hassles. Thus, for supply managers keeping up with organizational expectations is a daily grind in which long-term thinking is difficult to encourage. Moreover, significant problems are created for others in the organization, users or requisitioners, when their requirements are not fully met. Faulty materials, too large or too small quantities, late deliveries, high costs, inadequate service, and lack of continuity can all cause serious problems in certain areas of the organization. It is small wonder that many supply managers see as their prime objective the avoidance of these kinds of troubles. They consider themselves and their staff to be overworked and unappreciated. This is not exactly a prime environment to encourage long-term, opportunistic, and strategic thinking. And yet, that is exactly what this book is all about.

There is another side to supply (see Figure 1–2). This is the opportunistic, contribution or profit maximizing, strategic side. Supply is continually exposed to the needs of the organization on the one hand, and, on the other, to the marketplace. Therefore, it occupies a unique niche from which to identify opportunities for the organization which may not be apparent to others.

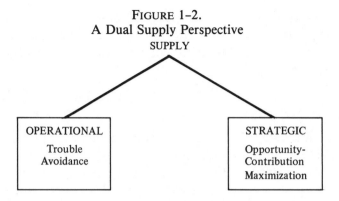

FIGURE 1-2.
A Dual Supply Perspective

SUPPLY CONTRIBUTION—THREE STAGES

In relation to organizational objectives and strategy, the supply function can occupy three different positions (see Figure 1-3). At its worst, it will be a negative factor in the sense that it prevents the achievement of objectives and thwarts strategies. In the neutral stage it is neither an obstruction nor an asset in the setting

FIGURE 1-3.
Three Stages of Supply Contribution
to Organizational Objectives and Strategy

Stage	Contribution	Top Management Involvement
1. Negative	Supply prevents the achievement of organizational objectives and strategies	Inadequate
2. Neutral	Supply neither an obstruction nor an asset in the achievement of organizational objectives and strategies	Sufficient to avoid problems
3. Positive	Supply a positive asset in planning, setting, and achievement of organizational objectives and strategies	Extensive to exploit opportunities

and achievement of organizational objectives and strategies. In the positive stage the supply function is an essential factor in the planning, setting, and achievement of organizational objectives and strategies.

The Negative Stage

In the negative stage the supply function is looked upon largely as a clerical function. Key decisions are made in the organization without due regard to the supply side. For example, marketing plans ignore supply considerations such as lead time, availability, and quality. New product introductions are planned and specifications drawn without supplier input, resulting in high costs or poor quality. Typical of the negative stage is suboptimizing behavior in which each department in the supply chain makes its own decisions in ignorance of the overall impact. The supply department may buy in large quantities to get a good price without due consideration of the inventory impact. Quality concerns are solely the responsibility of the quality assurance group and surface only after specifications have been frozen and vendors selected. There never seems to be enough lead time to do things right and, in the ensuing frustration, avoidance of blame is a key concern for the various parties involved.

In the negative stage there tends to be great concern over departmental territorial prerogatives: "Vendor selection and commercial concerns are my responsibility, accounting looks after payment, and engineering is totally responsible for specifications." Other typical comments include: "This is my budget and I can spend it anyway I like," and "It's too late to change anything now. Marketing says this is the only way to go."

Dwelling on the negative stage is unpleasant but not uncommon. Unfortunately, once an organization is mired in negative practices, considerable effort is necessary to lift it to a higher stage. Furthermore, the neutral stage will probably be impossible to avoid in the climb to the positive stage.

The Neutral Stage

In the neutral stage the undesirable aspects of the negative side have been addressed and eliminated. Frequently, the organization has gone to a materials management type of supply function in which purchasing, traffic, materials handling, inventory control, production planning and scheduling, receiving, and possibly quality control all report to a materials manager. Thus, at least, the most obvious undesirable trade-offs within the supply area itself can be addressed. Early involvement of the supply function and suppliers in new product or service development is not necessarily guaranteed, however, and supply considerations are not considered relevant in corporate strategy formulation, other than in a trouble avoidance context.

Many organizations currently seem to be in this neutral stage. Few managers outside the supply function and not all that many in the function itself are aware that opportunities exist to do significantly better by moving to the positive stage.

The Positive Stage

In the positive stage, supply is part of the competitive edge and of continuing top management concern. In fact, supply is fully integrated into the whole organization. Supply considerations are properly weighed by the other functional areas in the organization such as research and development, engineering, operations, finance, accounting, and human resources.

This positive stage requires not only that the supply function is staffed with high quality personnel, capable of identifying and exploiting major supply opportunities, but also that the other functions in the organization can and do support these efforts.

The greatest contribution potential for supply stems from early involvement in the development of new projects, products, services, and organizational strategies. A parallel exists on the engineering side. If the manufacturing engineer does not get a chance to consult with the design engineer before a design is fixed, the product may not be producible at the best quality or cost. The same principle applies to supply. Teamwork, consultation, coordination, and cooperation—these are the words that describe supply involvement in the positive stage.

It is probably much easier to slide back from the positive to the neutral stage than to move from the neutral to the positive, or to sustain a positive stage. Top management's efforts to assist the whole organization to achieve synergy will be vital in this positive stage.

Supply Benefits

This is an appropriate place to review briefly just exactly what the effective management of supply does have to offer. Bottom-line impact, information impact, and organizational morale and image impact are the three key areas that will be highlighted.

Bottom-Line Impact

In almost every organization, public or private, the supply function can significantly affect the bottom line. In the first place, the supply of goods and services to the organization may require a substantial percentage of the total budget or revenue of the organization. Very few organizations, public or private, spend less than about 20 or 30 percent of their total budget or revenue on the acquisition of goods and services from outside suppliers. For manufacturers in North America the average is over 60 percent of total revenue. Moreover, savings achieved in supply flow directly to the bottom line. For a typical manufacturer, a 5 percent overall saving in supply dollars may increase profits by 30 to 50 percent! (See Figure 1-4.) By the way, annual savings targets of 2 to 4 percent of purchase dollars are not uncommon.

Typically, the cost of operating and staffing the supply function is a small fraction—traditionally, in the 2 to 4 percent range—of what is spent by supply for purchases. It is therefore somewhat surprising that in some organizations the emphasis is on minimizing the supply department's budget, rather than the total dollars spent through supply. It is not at all unusual to find that extra dollars spent to improve the supply function generate an annual return of 500 to 1000 percent. (See Figure 1-5).

Direct and Indirect Bottom-Line Impact

Supply's impact on the bottom line can be both direct and indirect (see Figure 1-6). The most obvious direct impact is in terms of prices paid. If, without any change in specifications, quality, quantity, or delivery, the price or the laid-down cost for an acquired product or service can be lowered, the resulting saving goes directly to the bottom line. Most supply managers fully recognize this direct form of contribution. In many organizations such sav-

FIGURE 1-4.

The Impact of Supply Savings on the Bottom Line

A TYPICAL MANUFACTURER

Sales Revenue	$500,000,000
Total Purchases	320,000,000
Total Salaries and Wages	100,000,000
Financial and Other Costs	40,000,000
Profit Before Tax	40,000,000
5% Saving in Supply	16,000,000
Impact on Profitability	40% increase!

FIGURE 1-5.

The Cost of Supply and the Potential for Supply Savings

THE COST OF SUPPLY   THE POTENTIAL FOR SAVINGS·

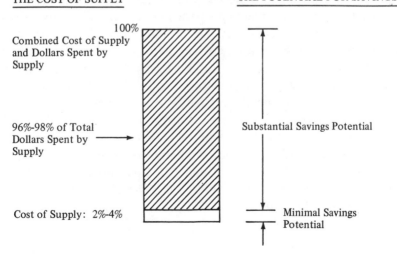

FIGURE 1-6.

The Bottom-Line Direct and Indirect Impact of Supply

BOTTOM-LINE IMPACT

DIRECT	INDIRECT
Savings in Dollars Spent by Supply	Savings in User Areas
Lower laid-down cost of goods and services acquired outside the organization (without changes in specifications)	Lower costs in user areas for materials, labor and overhead (including changes in specifications)
Through:	Through:
—negotiating lower prices and lower transportation costs —switching suppliers —combining purchases for greater clout —rationalization of vendors —giving suppliers better lead time and information —longer-term contracts —single sourcing —reverse marketing	—better quality —faster lead times —lower inventories —lower downtime —substitutions —simplification and standardization —value analysis —better supply systems —redesign —make or buy —reverse marketing

ings are regularly reported. Special programs to pursue such savings are a normal part of almost every supply unit. At United Technologies, for example, a recent program to pursue direct savings of this type had an objective of $1 million in savings per week.

Besides the total dollars spent for the acquisition of goods and services, there is a second impact on the bottom line, a bit more difficult to trace to its supply origin. Most organizational budgets are structured to reflect the standard realities of life in terms of quality, productivity, and inventory usage. Many quality and productivity problems have their origin in supply. And inventories are carried to cover up supply deficiencies. Improvement in supply performance in areas other than the actual price paid to suppliers can significantly affect the bottom line of the whole organization. Of course, it is difficult to estimate the amounts of indirect savings, but the total impact should exceed the direct savings potential in price reduction.

INFORMATION WINDOW

The supply function can be a valuable information resource because of its unique exposure to both organizational requirements and the world marketplace. The information gathered from current and potential suppliers, trade publications, and other purchasers can be of substantial value to others in the organization. For example, information on new technology and new products and services may be useful to operations and engineering as well as to marketing. Word of impending price changes, currency moves, government initiatives, and information about what other organizations or competitors are doing may be of concern to a wide range of executives and managers. A supply manager sensitive to the organization's objectives, strategies, and needs can perform a valuable role as an information seeker, sifter, and distributor.

ORGANIZATIONAL MORALE AND IMAGE

Everyone working for an organization is familiar with the consumer aspect of supply. This side is characterized by individual choice and ready availability of most items. Most employees find it extremely frustrating, therefore, if their own organization cannot provide quickly and efficiently what they can buy for themselves by just walking into a store. "What kind of a company am I working for, if it takes them three weeks to get me a red pencil?" is not an unreasonable question. In this context the supply function affects the morale of the people working inside the organization.

Supply also affects the corporation's image outside the organization in a variety of ways. Are local or domestic suppliers favored over others? Is the organizational buying stance in sympathy or in conflict with national government priorities? Are minority and small suppliers given a fair chance? Are suppliers chosen who are themselves environmentally and politically acceptable? Is the behavior of the supply staff ethical? Do suppliers who receive business react favorably to the way they are treated? Do suppliers who do not receive business feel they have been treated fairly? In fact, many procurement executives see supplier goodwill as a major corporate asset and something to be fostered assiduously.

Obviously, a well functioning supply organization can contribute in many other ways beyond the bottom-line, information, and image areas mentioned. In fact, it is somewhat surprising that the supply area has not received greater top management attention until now. Certainly the academic world must take its fair share of the blame. Very few universities and other institutions of higher learning have courses in administration or management that highlight the role of supply. Consequently, thousands of graduates each year enter the management world believing that what they have not been taught cannot be very important. Traditionally, the supply function has been seen as a clerical, rather than a strategic function, and has been staffed accordingly. Thus, the people within the supply function have themselves been unaware of the potential contribution they could make. In the last few decades, however, significant changes have been made.

In discussing his contacts for research into purchasing strategies, E. Raymond Corey of the Harvard Business School said:

> In studying at first hand the procurement operations they manage, I gained a great respect for the complexity of their work and the high degree of managerial skill it requires. In particular, I came to understand that procurement as a management function is undergoing considerable change, change that has been forced on it by events in the external environment. The Arab oil embargo, the shortages of 1972–73, the increasing government involvement in matters relating to procurement, the rapidly growing use of management information systems—a trend in big companies, generally, away from geographically decentralized structures—all these factors have had, and will continue to have, a profound effect on procurement strategies, organization, and decision-making processes.[4]

SUPPLY STRATEGY

The topic of supply or purchasing strategy is becoming better recognized, although in fact supply strategies have existed for a very long time. For example, vertical integration backward into supply sources has long been recognized as one way of expansion open to certain firms and certain industries.

Corey's text on this subject, cited above, includes a nu interesting case studies. His introductory comments to pur strategy follow:

> A strategy is a plan of action designed to achieve given goals and objectives. Both buyers and sellers have strategies for dealing with the other. The kinds of marketing strategy sellers develop and implement generally are well articulated within firms and in the literature. By contrast, procurement strategies—plans of action for obtaining supplies and for dealing with sellers— often are not clearly understood. Yet well-conceived and skillfully executed procurement strategies are highly critical to the success of any organization. Overall, an organization's growth and profitability will be affected greatly by its ability to secure supplies and to gain the benefits of new technologies from its supply sources.
>
> Procurement strategies vary so greatly from one purchasing situation to another because each situation is unique. Thus, every strategy has to be tailored to the type of product being purchased, the stage of the procurement cycle, the past purchasing history, the nature of the supply environment, and the buying company itself: its resources, its negotiating strength, and its purchasing policies.[5]

It is interesting that Corey underlines the idea that different organizations might use different supply strategies for different products under different circumstances. The idea that strategy is tailor-made for a specific procurement situation is a fundamental proposition.

The key question really is: How can the supply function contribute effectively to organizational objectives and strategy? And its companion: How can organizational objectives and strategies reflect opportunities and strengths in the supply area?

The ideal situation would be as shown in Figure 1–7. Ideally, objectives should be congruent with supply strategy and each in turn should be congruent with organizational objectives and organizational strategy. Although this diagram makes a lot of sense, it is difficult to achieve in reality.

In the first place, Figure 1–7 presupposes that organizational objectives are clearly identified and well known to everyone within the organization. The same applies to organizational strategy. This represents a tall order. The problem is that in the absence of such understanding, supply managers will start to substitute their own personal perceptions of what the organization is all about

FIGURE 1-7.
Congruence Between Supply and Organizational Strategies

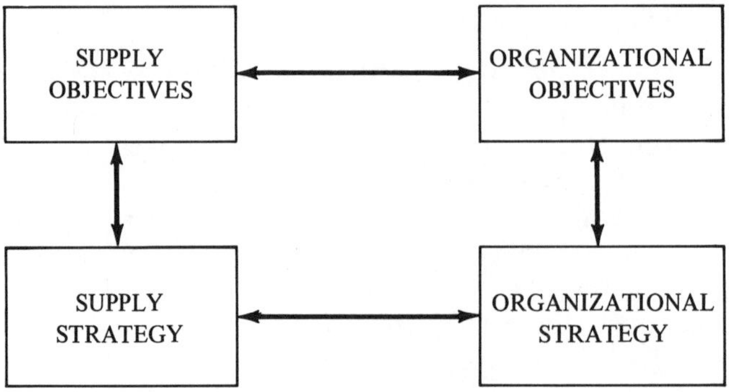

in place of the real ones. It would be truly exceptional if these perceptions were always correct.

Normal Organizational and Supply Objectives

Organizations normally pursue a variety of objectives. Four generally recognized ones include: (1) survival, (2) growth, (3) financial, and (4) environmental. It is normal for organizations to try to perpetuate themselves. The urge for survival tends to be strong, and few organizations will deliberately self-destruct on their own. Survival is, however, not a very ambitious objective for many organizations. Most tend to have a growth objective. There are many good reasons for this. Frequently, it is easier to manage an organization in a growth mode. Growth provides opportunities to advance, creates a positive morale, and presents new and interesting challenges. Financial objectives are ever present. For profit-making organizations these are often expressed as expected return on investment, profit levels, and cash flow expectations. For non-profit organizations and, particularly, government departments these may be expressed as deficit minimizing or budget limiting goals. Most organizations also include a variety of environmental objectives. These objectives do not only cover some of the traditional environmental concerns such as preservation of nature, clean air, land, and water. Organizations are also required to live within the laws of the country where they are located. Moreover, managers may be anxious to make sure their organization is seen as a "good citizen." Evidence of this may have to be given in terms of efforts to support government plans for the country and to respect cultural and societal views.

This simplified view of organizational objectives is not meant to imply that the process of setting, revising, and communicating them is a simple one. It is meant to show, however, that, given current supply objectives, a substantial amount of interpretation is required to translate organizational objectives into supply objectives.

At a very practical level normal supply objectives are identified as: (1) quality, (2) quantity, (3) delivery, (4) price, and (5) service. It is clear that failure to meet any one of these counts may create difficulties for the ultimate user of the product or service. Since the language of purchasing objectives is so different from that of corporate organizational ones the amount of interpretation the supply manager must provide is large. For example, in view of corporate objectives, what constitutes acceptable quality in a particular supply decision? It is quite possible that two supply managers faced with an identical set of circumstances might create different strategies to deal with them. Each might interpret the impact of corporate objectives and strategy differently. Also, each might have a different perception of the effectiveness of a certain type of supply strategy.

A different version of supply strategy is supplied in Figure 1–8. This shows supply strategy as matching current organizational needs to current market conditions and future needs to future market conditions. Since both needs and market conditions are likely to change over time, continued reassessment of the effectiveness of certain supply strategies is crucial.

FIGURE 1–8.
Supply Strategy: Fitting Needs to Markets, Short- and Long-Term

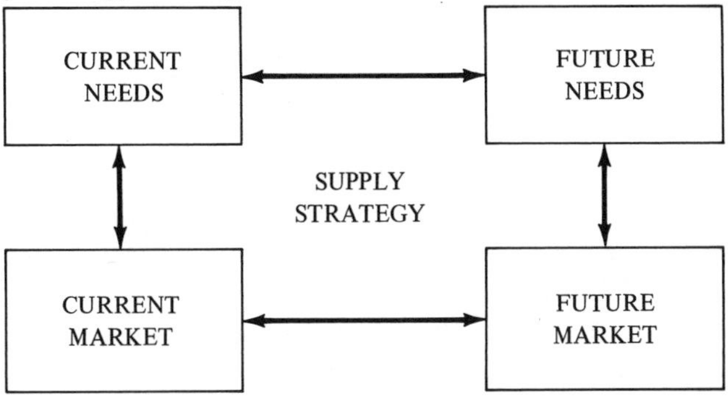

Supply Strategy Levels

Supply strategies can in fact be planned and executed at different levels. Level 1 could be at the organizational or corporate level. Level 2 would be at the supply department or supply unit level. Level 3 would bring it down to a product or service group. For example, what should our supply strategy be for paper? Level 4 would break it down to an individual product or service or to an individual purchaser. What should our supply strategy be for copy machine paper? Whenever possible, strategies between levels should be coordinated and congruent with one another. This of course requires a substantial amount of management and communication.

Supply Strategy—Options

An attempt will be made here to identify a few of the strategic options available in the various building blocks within a supply strategy. The elements chosen are the simple what, how much, who, when, what price, where, how, and why questions. For each, several options are identified for illustrative purposes. Clearly, these examples are not exhaustive.

WHAT.   There is a variety of ways to determine what needs to be supplied. The issue of what to make and what to buy is obviously a central one in the "what" consideration. The composition of supply requirements is a different aspect. Another component is the trade-off between leaning towards standard products and using special or custom-made ones. In the design of the organization's products, engineering can make a deliberate decision to try to design around standard available parts and materials, or it can seek specialty materials and designs. Such decisions have clear implications for the procurement strategy.

Make-or-Buy Decisions.   The make-or-buy decision represents a key strategic management option. Many supply managers are inclined to favor the buy option. Obviously the ability to buy effectively would be one factor favoring this option. Nevertheless, many other factors come into play. Most organizations develop attitudes towards this option over time and may tend to "lean" towards making or buying.

In the last decade in North America a tendency towards the

buying of services appears to be emerging. In both public and private organizations the contracting of services such as security, food, office and building and equipment maintenance, computer programming, data processing, engineering, and legal and accounting appears to be the trend. The use of limited-term contracts for various professional services may be attractive. Also, on the manufacturing side, the buy option is receiving more attention.

The make-or-buy question is particularly challenging for multiunit, multidivisional organizations in which certain units or divisions could be suppliers to others. The question of total corporate benefit versus unit profitability or performance needs to be examined with great care. Transfer pricing of trade between units is often a contentious issue. In multinational corporations, additional concerns in interunit trade center on tariffs, currency exchange, and political and tax issues.

Types of Purchases.   Most manufacturing organizations recognize different categories of purchases: raw materials, purchased parts, maintenance, repair, and operating (MRO) supplies, capital equipment, and services. For public organizations most supply is concerned with end-use requirements. Frequently, the supply department is subdivided into sections, each specializing in one of these categories. Practitioners believe that specialized expertise is required for each type of purchasing. Raw material supply often involves large-volume contracts, a thorough knowledge of primary processes, and high sensitivity to economics and the world supply situation. A buyer of raw materials is likely to specialize in relatively few items and would be expected to have a substantial amount of purchasing experience before being assigned to this task. By contrast, MRO supplies are often assigned to inexperienced buyers, because there are a large number of relatively small value items that are ordered repeatedly and often are sole sourced. Even in this category, items such as cleaning supplies, toweling, light bulbs, and so on would be seen as requiring less expertise than repair parts for production equipment.

Types of purchases may be further divided depending on whether they are repetitive or not. For repetitive purchases special care may be taken to ensure that a repeatable system of acquisition is designed. A totally different approach may have to be taken for nonrepetitive items.

A further division could be made according to the money spent on each type of purchase.

The ABC Concept. In most modern organizations the total number of individual items acquired can be very large. For example, at Syncrude (the world's largest producer of oil from tar sands, located in Northern Alberta, Canada), the total number of different line items exceeds 60,000. Clearly, this presents a tremendous acquisition problem. When viewed from a management perspective, it would not be wise to treat all items equally, or acquire them by the same system. One way to categorize total purchases is by separating according to the total dollar volume spent on each line item for a year. The "ABC" breakdown, derived from Pareto's law, would break total purchases into three categories, "A" items would normally represent about 10 percent of the total number of items acquired, but would account for about 70 percent of the total dollar volume. "B" items would represent about 20 percent of the total number of items and about 20 percent of the total dollar volume. "C" items, 70 percent of the total number, would account for approximately 10 percent of the total annual dollar volume. Since every one of the items is important to the continuing functioning of the total organization, availability of all must be assured. A totally different approach may be taken for "A" items, however, because of the high dollar volume they represent. "C" items can be safely stocked in sufficient quantities to avoid worrying about running out. Special delivery arrangements may have to be made for "A" items, because holding them in inventory would represent too large a drain on working capital. Similarly, if savings are sought, "A" items would represent a more fertile field of study than "B" or "C" items. It is also possible to categorize individual classes of purchases by the "ABC" concept. For example, raw materials, purchased parts, equipment, MRO supplies, and services can all be subclassified into "A," "B," and "C" items.

Thus, if the "ABC" concept is combined with types of purchases, and whether acquisition is repetitive or not, a three-dimensional block may be created as in Figure 1–9. The types of purchases are on the X axis and the "ABC" division on the Y axis with the repetitive–nonrepetitive division forming the Z axis. Such a combination would identify 30 different subsets, each of which might require specialized purchasing treatment.

HOW MUCH. The question of how much should be bought at any one time has tremendous implications for inventory con-

FIGURE 1-9.
Organization of Purchases

AXIS	DIMENSION
X	Raw Materials, Purchased Parts, MRO Supplies, Equipment, Services
Y	A, B, C
Z	Repetitive, Nonrepetitive

trol. The old-fashioned view was that quantity discounts might be obtained only if one purchased very large requirements at a time. This often led to substantial inventory investment. The more modern view leans toward taking very small deliveries at a time, just enough to meet current requirements, but to try to obtain price advantages through longer-term and quantity commitments.

WHO.   Who should be doing the buying for the organization? Should the buying function be centralized? What quality of staff should go into this department if buying is centralized? Most organizations continue to struggle with these questions. The simple answer is that without centralization purchasing has no clout. Also, without qualified staff the function can perform little more than clerical routines. An accompanying question to these issues is the degree to which top management involvement should be used in strategy formulation and execution. Frequently, purchasers are anxious to show that they can do a good job on their own, and may fear to ask for top management assistance when, in fact, it might be essential.

WHEN.   When to buy has major implications for delivery performance and also for cash planning. For certain commodities the decision whether to forward buy or not may be the only option of influencing the price paid. Anyone who has followed the price of gold during the last ten years will appreciate this.

WHAT PRICE.   It is possible for an organization to develop a specific price strategy. An organization may deliberately decide to pay premium prices, but to expect outstanding supplier performance on other counts. Some organizations may set their price target at market standard, others may wish to have extremely aggressive price expectations.

The three major approaches to price determination are: (1) cost-based, (2) market-based, and (3) competition-based.

Cost-Based Approach.   One supply strategy is to pursue a cost-based approach wherever possible. The assumption here is that the purchaser would be sufficiently familiar with the cost of producing the material, product, or service in question so as to be able to negotiate a reasonable price based on anticipated cost. A vendor would be told what cost-based price has to be met, and failure to agree on a specific price target would remove the supplier from further consideration. Such a cost-based strategy would require a number of skilled purchasing analysts, extensive engineering and accounting support, and strong negotiation skills. The automotive and appliance companies have used these strategies extensively with their suppliers. Since the purchaser has just as much information as the supplier on the technology and the various costs of manufacture, the idea that the purchaser might make rather than purchase the product is an ever present one with a cost-based strategy.

Market-Based Approach.   Market-based supply strategies would recognize that the price is set by factors beyond the purchaser's or vendor's control. A typical example is when prices are set by government decree. Other examples would include prices for commodities where no vendor or purchaser is so large as to unduly influence market price. Under these circumstances, only the decision of when to buy may have an impact on the actual price paid. Also, it might be possible to negotiate for extra services without changing the price.

Competition-Based Approach.   Another supply strategy for price may be competition-based. The assumption here is that sufficient competition exists to establish a competitive price. Vendors might be asked to bid on an organization's requirements. Presumably, the hungriest vendor would win the contract.

Certain organizational constraints or vendor marketing practices may make it impossible for a purchaser to pursue a preferred price strategy for a particular product or service. Therefore, it is probably proper to talk in terms of leaning in a certain direction, rather than implying that the purchaser has completely free choice to pursue one strategy or another. If goods are priced on a market-based philosophy the purchaser's options are clearly limited. The major choice facing the purchaser, therefore, is whether to lean towards a cost-based strategy or a competition-based one.

WHERE.   Where to buy also has strategic implications. A first cut is geographical. Should the organization purchase locally or regionally? Frequently, the local business community has a ready answer to this question. Local managers are often exposed to considerable pressure to purchase from local suppliers. On a larger scale the question evolves to whether to purchase domestically or internationally. This is an issue of interest to governments.

A different dimension of the "where" question concerns the size of suppliers preferred. Should the organization seek out large or small suppliers, and for what reasons? A different dimension again involves multiple versus single sourcing; yet another whether a high or low supplier turnover is desirable. What are the desired supplier relationships that make sense for the buying organization? Whether to exclude certain vendors from quoting may be part of the decision whether a supplier certification program makes sense or does not. Frequently, governments find it difficult to exclude vendors from the right to bid. In the aerospace industry supplier certification is an absolute must and only approved suppliers are allowed to participate in the battle for a customer's business.

HOW.   There is a large variety of ways in which the supply strategy can actually be executed. How the manager attempts to achieve objectives will become evident in the choice of actual purchasing systems and techniques. A wide choice is available as the following examples indicate. The choice of systems and procedures for the various phases in the acquisition process is great.

Computer-based systems provide opportunities to supply information and perform tasks heretofore thought impossible. Whether to use negotiation, competitive bids, fixed bids, public opening of bids, or other ways of securing prices is largely left to the industrial purchaser. The governmental purchaser is required to follow more prescribed rules. The purchaser may wish to go for blanket orders or open orders. Systems contracting has provided an opportunity to get both quick delivery and good prices with a minimum of record keeping. The Kaiser check system affords the supplier an opportunity to get paid at the moment of order shipment, because a blank check is attached to the purchase order.

Group buying, particularly attractive in the public sector, allows small units to combine to obtain the benefits from pooled requirements. Materials Requirements Planning consists of a computerized system for handling dependent demand items and ties suppliers very closely to production schedules. Long-term contracts afford an opportunity to commit suppliers to future deliveries. The organization's position on ethics may encourage or discourage the use of certain practices.

WHY.   The specific strategy chosen in the first place has to be justified on the basis that it makes supply objectives congruent with organizational objectives. Actually, there may be market reasons for choosing a specific strategy. If it is standard practice in a certain industry to conduct business a certain way, this may be sufficient reason in itself for the purchaser to conform. Internal reasons specific to the purchasing organization may be relevant. For example, an outstanding engineering group, current with new technology, may encourage the organization to pursue a strategy of specialized, custom-made materials and parts and the cost-based approach. On the other hand, an inexperienced and poorly qualified purchasing staff may force the organization to lean towards making rather than buying, because the supply department's skills are not a particular asset to the organization.

The richness and variety of strategic options must be evident, even from this list which represents nothing but a sample of the choices really available. Any experienced practitioner would have no difficulty adding dozens of other options.

The key issue from the standpoint of this book is that these various strategic options may be exercised in a passive, reactive, unplanned fashion, or in an aggressive, proactive, planned manner.

Good Suppliers

The supplier selection decision has traditionally been seen as the key in sound supply management. Presumably, the right supplier will make sure that the customer receives exactly what is required. Therefore, time and effort spent on locating the right source will be fully justified in the returns.

What is a good supplier? A good supplier lives up to the deal made with respect to quality, quantity, delivery, price, and service. A better supplier goes well beyond this minimum by taking the initiative to suggest ways and means whereby the customer can improve products, services, and processes. An exceptional supplier places the customer's needs first and is in tune with the long-range objectives and strategies of the customer. The exceptional supplier has the mission to make the customers prosper. Good, better, and exceptional suppliers are scarce. Therefore, supply management can be called the battle for good suppliers.

If a good supplier is found, it is wise for the customer to hang on. Every supplier switch is costly. The support of exceptional suppliers allows an organization to undertake its programs and strategies with even greater confidence. The managers know they are part of a larger team.

To a large extent, suppliers are only as good as they have to be. Therefore, if the demands placed on suppliers are not exacting, it is possible for the supplier to survive with relatively mediocre performance. It is interesting that many supply managers believe a supplier is good when it delivers on time. In fact, the term "great service" has come to mean on-time delivery instead of the extra attention, support, and advice the supplier provides along with good quality, right quantity, on-time delivery, and a fair price. We deserve the suppliers we have because we have not asked for more.

There is a way in which the battle for good suppliers can be won without scratching other customers away from a desired source. Good, better, and exceptional suppliers can be created over time using reverse marketing.

LIVING IN A WORLD DOMINATED BY MARKETERS

North America, in particular, represents the geographical area in the world most dominated by the marketing viewpoint. The art of marketing has been honed to a very fine skill and the marketing area has for many years continued to attract some of the brightest and most aggressive people in our society. It might be an easy assumption that in such a world the need for expertise in buying is minimal, that the marketers will look after the customers. Actually, nothing could be farther from the truth.

As marketing dominance has continued to grow, the need for a countervailing force to protect the needs of the buying organization has become increasingly apparent. In the supply context, it makes no sense to have a high school graduate attempting to cope with a bright MBA sales representative. All marketing plans are ultimately based on the needs of the selling organization. Supply plans give first priority to the needs of the buying organization. This, in turn, creates the need for reverse marketing.

THE TRADITIONAL VIEW OF SUPPLY

In the traditional view of supply, the purchaser responds to the marketing efforts of current and potential suppliers. (See Figure 1-10.)

In this context, the initiative is with the supplier, not the purchaser. There are excellent reasons why the supplier likes to have

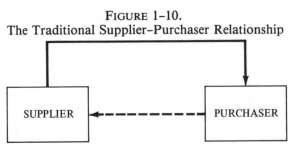

FIGURE 1-10.
The Traditional Supplier–Purchaser Relationship

The supplier tries to persuade the purchaser to buy.

it this way. Long experience has shown the marketer that the aggressor tends to have the upper hand. It is the supplier's needs that are foremost in the marketer's plans and actions. Taking the initiative forces one to do one's homework. When the proposal under consideration is the supplier's, the purchaser is forced into a predetermined perspective and role.

Even though a sound marketing plan is supposed to be built on the satisfying of the customer's needs, it is always prepared with satisfaction of the supplier's needs as the primary objective. More will be said about this later.

Even within this traditional context of marketing and procurement, a traditional role for purchaser aggressiveness has been reserved.

> Products or parts that have not previously been made, intricacies of special design, unusual requirements in the specification or different conditions and use, and the utilization of unfamiliar materials for which there is little precedent in treatment and fabrication are some of the factors that may lead to a situation for which no established supply source stands ready at hand. Or, from the standpoint of practical procurement, the only available sources may be too distant, prices may be exorbitant or out of line with budgeted costs for the product, production capacity may already be fully occupied so that no new customers may be accommodated, or the potential suppliers may simply be unwilling or uninterested in additional business. Under any of these circumstances, the buyer's responsibility is not to select but to create a satisfactory source.[6]

Thus, if the current market is incapable of meeting quality, quantity, delivery, price, and service objectives, the purchaser may well be forced to develop new sources of supply.

In this traditional context, the reverse marketing decision has a connotation of last resort or one of no choice. The purchaser would really prefer to select rather than create sources. However, circumstances do not permit the first option.

This is a fully legitimate reason for engaging in reverse marketing. And, regardless of the motive, most of what follows in this book is pertinent to this form of reverse marketing out of necessity. It implies a vision of a buyer firmly anchored to chair, desk, terminal or computer, telex, FAX, and telephone. It implies a great reluctance to leave this cocoon of buying efficiency to venture forth on a distasteful mission with low probability of success.

THE BROADER VIEW OF REVERSE MARKETING

The traditional view restricts the scope of reverse marketing unnecessarily. Reverse marketing should represent an option when other choices are available. And the reason it should be preferred is because better results are expected from its use.

The example of value analysis, and its origin, may illustrate what is meant. Harry Ehrlicher who was in charge of the supply function at General Electric during World War II noticed a curious phenomenon. Shortages of parts and materials were normal occurrences during wartime. Many items were considered vital to the military effort and others were simply not available. Harry Ehrlicher noted that when such shortages did occur, the solution found, whether it involved redesign or a substitute part or material, often represented an improvement on the original design, part, or materials specified. Curious as to why this would happen, when one would normally expect the opposite result of poorer quality or higher cost, Ehrlicher decided he would some day try to take a hard look at it. It was not until the high postwar demand for consumer products had abated that Ehrlicher saw his chance. In 1948 he was able to enlist the assistance of Larry Miles to conduct a formal investigation into this phenomenon and what caused it. Larry Miles came up with the answer. When we have no choice but to take action on a procurement problem, we are forced to reexamine the basic need and the various ways in which this need can be satisfactorily met. Such a systematic approach to need definition and its satisfaction almost invariably yields better results than the original design or specification. He termed his systematic approach "value analysis." Harry Ehrlicher was delighted. He wanted to take the next step. If it worked so well during war when we had no choice, why not use it during peace, when there is a choice?

The same argument applies to reverse marketing. Research has shown that purchasers tend to get surprisingly good results when they engage in reverse marketing, prodded on by the reality that they really had no other choice. If reverse marketing works so well when the purchaser uses it out of necessity, why not use it when choices are available? As was the case in value analysis, further research has shown that there is no need to restrict the use of reverse marketing to those instances of no choice. It works equally well at other times.

Figure 1–11.
Reverse Marketing

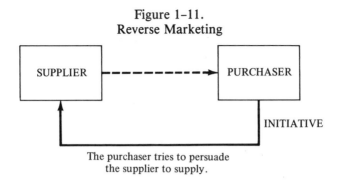

The purchaser tries to persuade
the supplier to supply.

Graphically, reverse marketing can be represented as in Figure 1–11. The simple reversal of arrows from Figure 1–10 produces a substantially different perspective. The purchaser, instead of being persuaded to buy, now tries to persuade the supplier to provide!

In reverse marketing the purchaser is aware that benefits will accrue to both the supplier and the purchaser, benefits of which the supplier may not be aware. These benefits may be limited to the particular order at hand, or they may include quality, technical, systems, marketing, financial, and management assistance; future business from the same purchaser as well as from others; training; reduction of marketing efforts; sharing of information permitting smoother manufacturing levels and a minimum of inventory; and so on.

REASONS FOR REVERSE MARKETING

There are many reasons why a purchaser may want to engage in reverse marketing. These include the traditional reasons put forth by Heinritz and Farrell mentioned above and can be expanded with the following:

1. High payoffs
2. Market deficiencies
3. Future considerations
4. Social, political, geographical, and environmental concerns
5. Technology
6. Recognition and appreciation
7. Current trends

High Payoffs

Reverse marketing is for the ambitious and the greedy. It suits those who are interested in more than what the market is willing or seemingly able to offer. High payoffs are possible because the purchaser has been forced to do the proper homework. As in value analysis, careful attention to the purchaser's needs as a starting point assures that priorities, options, and objectives can be well established. By taking the initiative with the supplier, the purchaser assures that it is the purchasing proposal that becomes the focus of the discussion. Whether the goal is a substantially improved quality performance, a larger or smaller quantity than usual, a significant price or cost reduction, greatly improved delivery performance, extended service support or terms of payment, or any combination, reverse marketing should be seriously considered. And, the more exceptional or unusual the objectives are from the supplier's perspective, the greater the need for using reverse marketing becomes. Most standard procurement tools and techniques have been developed for the traditional marketing-procurement context. In that context well-honed marketing tools and concepts prevent purchasing from obtaining too large a slice. As the examples in the following chapters show, the potential improvement in value represents results worthy of the extra procurement and other organizational resources required.

Although reverse marketing does not need to be confined to the high-value, high-volume "A" requirements, it is here that the largest potential exists. Somebody once asked an English bank robber why he robbed banks. The reply "That's where the money is" applies to reverse marketing as well. It is a custom tool to be applied to custom situations where the payoff warrants the initial investment in time and effort.

All research results show that very high payoffs are possible whether these be in quality, quantity, delivery, price, service, or other areas. The examples in this book will document a number of specific examples and the results achieved.

Marketing and Market Deficiencies

There are bound to be deficiencies in the normal marketing-procurement process in which the marketer traditionally takes the initiative. At the extreme, neither party may realize the other exists. Even when an ongoing relationship does exist, neither marketer nor buyer may be fully aware of each other's strengths and weaknesses, needs, opportunities, and problems. The marketer's perception of the purchaser's needs may be incorrect and the purchaser may not be aware of this, or vice versa.

Lack of appreciation of each other's needs and opportunities might arise because of salesperson and/or buyer specialization, a lack of aggressiveness by the salesperson, or a lack of inquisitiveness by the purchaser. Often a vendor may put marketing emphasis on selected products in its line, possibly for historical or profit margin reasons. The neglected segments of the product line may be the ones which the purchaser needs to solve a problem or to prevent a future problem from arising. When one or a few companies dominate an industry so as to restrict competition, the development of another source of supply may be necessary to improve prices.

Future Considerations

It is relatively easy for both supplier and purchaser to slip into a mode where both are concerned primarily with satisfying the current requirements and spend little time on future needs. This puts the onus on the purchaser to determine what future procurement needs will be. Questions such as the following should be addressed:

- What plans does the organization have to meet its future goals?
- How does supply fit in with these plans?
- Will it be necessary to create new sources to meet future supply needs?

Familiarity with the organization's long-range plans is a prerequisite to effective procurement planning. Without extensive discussion between purchaser and supplier, it is unrealistic to expect the supplier to predict accurately what the purchaser's future supply needs are likely to be and to take unilateral action to meet these needs well. Similarly, it is naive to assume that whatever form the purchaser's future needs may take, the market will automatically be able to take care of these.

With the ever-changing environment, future supply needs may be quite different from current ones, and the onus will be on the purchaser to develop suppliers to meet these needs.

Social, Political, Geographical, and Environmental Concerns

Often, there are reasons other than purely short-term economic ones why it is good business to develop suppliers. Governmental regulations—federal, state, and municipal—may not only encourage, but dictate the development of local and/or minority suppliers. Import substitution, foreign exchange limitations, offset agreements, and local unemployment conditions may require local reverse marketing. Geographical conditions and distances from markets may make long supply lines unrealistic. An organization may wish to be seen as a good corporate citizen. With increasing emphasis being placed on the environment and good corporate citizenship, the desirability of doing business with a supplier who has a good reputation for respecting the environment may well result in developing new sources of supply.

An interesting example of local reverse marketing arose when a mining company was in the process of establishing the viability of a highly promising ore body in a remote location. The purchasing manager insisted that the crews in the field purchase all their requirements from the merchants in the nearest town. It might have been cheaper to outfit the crews with food and other requirements from the large city hundreds of miles away. However, it turned out that to get the ore out the feasibility study showed two main options. One was to build a trestle through the center of the small town. The other was to bypass the town at an increased cost of over $20 million. The town council voted in favor of the through-town route. It is, of course, impossible to credit the purchasing manager's decision with this outcome. However, it is easy to see how the small merchants on the town's council might have voted had the big mining company taken the lower-cost supply option.

Technology

Technological changes, both inside the purchaser's organization and in the marketplace, may well initiate reverse marketing. The purchaser's needs may change and new vendors may have to be found. If the purchaser is in the high-technology field, the ability to predict which vendors will be capable of bringing new technology on-stream first, and which will survive, and the ability to make these educated guesses pay off, may be essential for the survival and growth of the purchaser's firm. Sewing up potential sources before the competition gets to them may be the goal of the reverse marketing effort.

New technology changes the economic relationships in design trade-offs and substitutions may come from totally different industries. Just a few trade-off examples include: plastics versus metal, paper versus plastics, electronic versus mechanical, liquids versus solids, synthetics versus natural products, paper versus paperless, truck versus train, plane versus boat, instant versus delayed, on-line versus batch, and machine versus human. New technology often allows new suppliers to enter the market and old suppliers to die ungracefully. Clearly, no well-run organization can sit idle while these changes abound. To operate effectively in a world in which technology changes abound, reverse marketing may well have to be practiced extensively.

Recognition and Appreciation

Top management often perceives supply as performing a passive role, being reactive to problems immediately at hand rather than proactive to internal demands and external happenings. Ammer[7] has stated that "management of many companies not only accept but actually encourage what can be called 'passive' purchasing." Purchasing has been described as being "administrative" rather than "strategic." Involvement in meaningful reverse marketing can help to overcome this stigma.

Normally, top management gets involved in the supply function only when something goes wrong. However, the development of new sources of supply has to be sold as an opportunity to top management and others in the organization. This involvement gives supply more visibility and a better profile within the organization. The very act of suggesting projects with potentially high payoff for others in the organization will tend to bring supply into a more positive role.

Current Trends

Reverse marketing is congruent with a number of current trends. These include the trends toward greater emphasis on quality, international trade, just-in-time production and delivery, Materials

Requirements Planning, integrated vendor-purchaser systems, systems contracting, vendor rationalization, legislative requirements, and greater value for the purchase dollar. It is not necessary to discuss each of these in detail. Before a purchaser settles on a single source, however, it is obvious that a tremendous amount of work may be required in the quality, just-in-time, and systems areas, to name just a few, before a truly effective supply system has been achieved. The continued pressure for better value stems from severe budget limitations as well as the growing realization that traditional sources of funding such as tax or sales revenues may not grow at historical rates. As the more standard approaches towards savings in the procurement area have already been exhausted, the growing need to turn to new and more powerful concepts reinforces the usefulness of reverse marketing.

On the quality side, most purchasers have found that banging their fists on the table tends to produce limited results. Vendors may have to be assisted in quality assurance and control programs that address the purchaser's specific needs. Moreover, the work does not stop there. Such work may have to be extended to the supplier's suppliers and so on down the chain. This adds up to a formidable task of reverse marketing.

Obviously, more reasons than just these seven exist. Reverse marketing is good for the morale of the procurement people who become involved in it. One successful effort encourages another. It identifies strengths and weaknesses in both the purchaser's and supplier's organization, it is a good training and communications means, it forces purchasers to expand their horizons and do a better job of preparing for future needs, it changes the mission of the supply function to fit properly with the organization's priorities.

The reality is not whether reverse marketing should be undertaken or not. It is a matter of how much, when, where, and how. The examples in the following chapters will substantiate the argument that reverse marketing is valuable, illustrating the phenomenon in action.

REVERSE MARKETING AND PURCHASING RESEARCH

Purchasing research has as a primary objective the facilitation of better purchasing decision making through the use of research techniques. This often requires a careful analysis of the future and how it will impact on decisions that must be made today. Where does the purchaser's organization expect to be in the future? What product lines or services will it provide? And what is the availability of the needed resources? These are precisely the types of questions that are raised in a reverse marketing context. Both purchasing research and reverse marketing are future oriented with long range planning as a common key. Purchasing research, therefore, complements the reverse marketing effort to reveal the desirability and feasibility of specific development projects.

Reverse marketing and value analysis/engineering are similarly related and complementary. The detection of value improvement opportunities is the primary objective of value analysis/engineering. In reverse marketing, these opportunities may be of benefit to the supplier as well. Value engineering often requires extensive work with specialty suppliers, perfect grist for the reverse marketing mill. However, reverse marketing is not always an accompaniment to value analysis; it may result from recommendations arising out of value analysis, or it may not. Unlike value analysis, its purpose is the development of a source of supply; like value analysis, it may result in substantial savings to the purchaser.

REVERSE MARKETING AND THE MAKE-OR-BUY DECISION

The relationship between reverse marketing and the decision to make or buy is similar to the purchasing research relationship, in that both may generate the need for reverse marketing. The make-or-buy decision is a complement to rather than a substitute for reverse marketing. Anyone engaged in the preparatory work of reverse marketing must do cost, product, and process analyses, market and feasibility studies, and so on. It is only logical that the purchaser should ask the question: "If it is a great business opportunity for the vendor, could it be one for my organization?" or the reverse.

The other side of the make-or-buy decision is the persuasion of people within the purchaser's own organization to make or buy the item in question. This exercise is similar to persuading a supplier to supply.

THE REVERSE MARKETING DECISION

The choice of whether or not to engage in reverse marketing should be based on a sound analysis of the alternatives available. Some of the options may be:

1. Maintain the status quo
2. Change suppliers
3. Make own
4. Do reverse marketing
5. A combination of the above

These alternatives should be assessed carefully. The objective is to select the alternative giving the best payoff for the time, money, and effort involved.

The reverse marketing decision involves the evaluation of many opportunity costs. The resources used to develop one source could have been used elsewhere in the organization with a corresponding payoff there. Therefore, the decision not to engage in reverse marketing presumes that another alternative will result in a greater overall benefit to the organization.

BRIEF SUMMARY

1. Reverse marketing is an aggressive, imaginative approach which requires a strategic perspective of the supply role in the organization.

2. In reverse marketing the purchaser takes the initiative rather than the vendor.

3. Reasons for reverse marketing include: the potential high payoffs; market deficiencies; future considerations; social, political, geographical, or environmental considerations; technology; organizational recognition; fit with organizational objectives and strategies; and congruence with current trends in materials management such as the renewed concerns for quality and value, international trade; just-in-time and material requirements planning; integrated purchaser-vendor systems, and legislative requirements.

4. Reverse marketing may involve current, past, or new suppliers for any kind of existing or new product or service.

5. Reverse marketing complements such procurement techniques and concepts as value analysis and purchasing research.

6. The use of reverse marketing may be out of necessity or by choice.

7. Both public and private organizations can use reverse marketing to increase supply effectiveness.

8. Reverse marketing is best illustrated by Figure 1–11.

CHAPTER 2

The Reverse Marketing Framework

REVERSE marketing can be seen as a process, or a sequence of steps, initiated by the purchaser with the aim of achieving a specific supply objective. Thus far, discussion of reverse marketing has largely centered on its rationale. The time has come to take a hard look at what it actually entails. How is it practiced? A detailed example will be presented here and subsequently analysed. It will become apparent that a framework can be applied. The reverse marketing process can be seen to contain a series of distinct and chronologically sequential phases. The understanding of these phases and why they are necessary is an essential precondition to successful execution.

CASE: MALSTON BAKERY INC.

John Thomas, Director of Purchases of the Malston Bakery, felt that an important part of his role in the firm was to monitor major raw materials and supplies to determine if the best possible value was being received. Simultaneously, he searched for opportunities to assure long-term value for these requirements. John had become increasingly concerned about the cost-price squeeze of the company's bread lines.

Malston Bakery produced many different kinds of bread, rolls, cakes, and packaged biscuits. It operated three bakeries in different cities several hundred miles apart. Annual sales exceeded $200 million, of which bread sales amounted to about $30 million. Malston had been established for about 100 years and had an enviable reputation for high-quality products sold under a variety of well-known brand names. The company had been profitable since its inception and had never incurred a loss. Its finances had been conservatively managed and it had no outstanding debt.

Purchasing

The purchasing department at Malston was responsible for all purchases made by the organization. John Thomas, its director, was responsible for all materials-related functions in the firm, which included a centralized purchasing department for the three bakeries. Major dollar items included: (1) raw materials and packaging, and (2) delivery trucks and equipment. John Thomas reported to Bill Simmons, the president of the firm.

Bread

Even though bread sales amounted to a significant portion of total sales, profitability on bread had not kept pace with the other lines sold by the company. Tough competition had kept prices down, but ingredient and packaging costs had risen considerably, squeezing margins alarmingly. Currently, flour costs represented 55 percent of the total cost of producing bread. John Thomas believed that flour prices were unreasonably high, but all efforts on his part to negotiate lower prices with his existing vendors had failed. He was, therefore, wondering what other alternatives were open to him.

In one of his frequent discussions with the president, Bill Simmons, he found a sympathetic ear.

> BILL: John, I see from your latest monthly report that you're concerned about the way the price of bread flour keeps increasing every month. I don't need to tell you what kind of a ridiculous competitive situation we have in the marketplace today. Profit margins are low to start with and we are being squeezed by higher material costs, and, as you pointed out in your report, flour costs in particular. Every increase in the cost of flour substantially reduces our profit. What can we do about it?

JOHN: I know what you mean. I see you have the latest price forecast sheet—I sure didn't like handing it in. We have half a dozen flour suppliers and it seems strange to me that each month they come in with new prices, all identical; they go up together. When I try to negotiate, I can't get them to budge.

Flour was purchased on a hand-to-mouth basis at Malston because government regulations required it could not be purchased more than 60 days in advance. Deliveries were made daily. The purchasing agent in charge of raw material buying, Dick Grindlay, consulted frequently with John Thomas about flour purchases. When both of them discussed the president's concern, they reviewed all of their past efforts and tried to come up with some new ideas. When neither was able to suggest anything reasonable, John Thomas came to the following conclusion:

Maybe part of our problem is that we just don't know enough about what is happening out there in the industry. Perhaps we should just go right back to basics and find out what is happening to our suppliers. It's just possible that if we talk to enough people, we might get some new insights and some new ideas. Even if no revolutionary ideas evolve, the whole exercise itself will give us a better insight into the milling business and impress our concerns on our existing suppliers.

Dick Grindlay agreed, but was concerned that he himself had too many projects on the go to be able to take any significant time off.

To that John Thomas answered:

For me, this issue is significant enough that I'm just going to have to make time available to take a harder look at it. If we don't get going on this matter now, we'll just keep going on the way we have been in the past, and I don't think we can live with that kind of situation forever.

When John Thomas raised the idea of visiting the various suppliers in the industry, Bill Simmons had second thoughts.

BILL: Do you really believe that you can find an answer to the increasing flour costs out there in the boondocks? Why don't you just invite a few flour mill sales managers into your office and ask them what is going on with their pricing?

JOHN: I do that all the time—at least once each month when they come with their price increases. I keep a daily record of market prices of wheat and also for mill feeds. When feed prices are strong and wheat prices are steady, I push them for a decrease; sometimes I get some concessions, but they're only small and they're given most reluctantly. What I don't understand is how the smaller mills can justify the same kinds of price increases as the larger mills. That is one of the questions I need answered.

BILL: I have no better suggestions myself. I like the idea of having a good look at what they're up to on their home ground. Good luck!

Visits to the Mills

During the following two months, John visited each of the six mills currently supplying bread flour to Malston. The meetings with personnel at the various mills had been informative and John felt that he had gained considerable insight into the flour milling business. At each mill, he had made it a point to ask for a detailed tour of all the facilities and also to discuss the business of flour milling with the top marketing and operations executives in the firm and, if possible, also with the chief executive. The credit manager at Malston had been able to obtain financial statements on several of the mills. On the basis of all of the information available to him, John Thomas had come to the conclusion that the investment in equipment and the labor costs of milling did not warrant the high margins the suppliers were getting. He still did not yet have a satisfactory way of counteracting the price increases, however.

A Cost-Price Formula

The president of one of the mills visited had mentioned to John Thomas the notion of a cost-price formula. The idea was relatively simple. It recognized that the mill had to acquire its raw material, wheat, at certain prices. In the process of milling, the miller incurred certain labor and other costs. The miller received extra income for the by-products of the milling process sold to feed companies. Finally, to give the mill a satisfactory return on its investment and to cover its various overheads, an additional contribution percentage had to be applied. When John Thomas pressed for further details, the president claimed he was in no position to provide the material instantaneously, but he would send it along in the mail. Several weeks after this visit, John Thomas received a copy of the proposed formula. He checked it over carefully, but the net result was that the price the company wanted was just as high as that of any of the other competitors. He did believe, however, that the idea of a formula was intriguing and might have some merit provided a better total price could be received.

The Ross Mill

Malston also produced soft cake and cookie products. The flour used in these items was made with winter wheat, which required different treatment from bread flour which was made from higher protein hard wheat. Annual purchases of soft wheat flour (made from winter wheat) amounted to $13.2 million per year. The principal supplier of soft wheat flour was a small mill owned and operated by the two Ross brothers, Dave and Fred. The Ross Mill had been a long-term quality supplier of soft wheat only. There were no government controls on soft wheat flour. The two brothers had approached John Thomas six months earlier and inquired whether Malston would be interested in buying their flour mill. They were both getting along in age and did not feel they had sufficient capital to make the necessary improvements to the mill to keep ahead of new developments. John Thomas had taken the matter to Bill Simmons for consideration and following an examination of the mill by an outside consultant, the Malston board of directors decided against the purchase, stating that the mill was obsolete. Recently, the Ross brothers had sold the mill to an entrepreneur, Peter Hellibell. John noted in his appointment book that he had already scheduled an introductory meeting with Dave Ross and Peter Hellibell to discuss the new ownership.

Peter Hellibell made a good impression on John Thomas during the first visit. Peter explained he had major expansion plans for the Ross Mill for the next five years, which included tripling its capacity. Because Peter Hellibell was new at flour milling, he planned to keep the Ross brothers on for technical advice and assistance. Apparently, Peter Hellibell had invested most of his ready cash in the initial purchase of the mill and was trying to raise additional capital from outside sources.

Bread Flour Alternatives

John pondered the options he had before him with respect to his bread problem. His attempts at negotiating price reductions with his suppliers had proved next to futile and his ongoing talks with potential suppliers suggested to him that their prices would follow the same pattern as that of Malston's current suppliers. Malston had investigated getting into the milling business itself through the purchase of the Ross Mill and the board of directors had decided against that move. He was particularly concerned that none of these conventional alternatives appeared to have enough merit at this time. Continuing to push on one or the other, or all, might just waste time and eventually result in an acceptance of the status quo.

John wondered whether Peter Hellibell might be interested in quicker expansion of his Ross Mill by entering into the bread flour milling business. Such an alternative might give Malston the leverage it needed with the traditional flour suppliers. At the same time, it would permit Hellibell to expand at a faster rate than he anticipated. If Peter Hellibell needed the assurance of Malston business as a way of obtaining the necessary financing, Malston might be in a position to work out a pricing agreement advantageous to both sides. John wondered if the cost-price formula concept might not be applied to this situation.

As he reflected on the potential this alternative might hold for him, John Thomas began to see the advantages for both sides in a clearer light. He also felt that unless the deal was of sufficient magnitude, it would not be worth the time and effort for either side to get seriously involved. He therefore set a price target for the Ross Mill product at 7 percent below market price. This percentage spread would have to be maintained for a sufficiently long period to enable Malston to lever its existing suppliers to the lower level. At this stage, John was not too sure what total volumes and length of contract might have to be for it to be sufficiently interesting for both sides. John recognized that a move such as pursuing the Ross Mill represented an unusual venture for Malston. Normally, Malston would only deal with established suppliers. In this case, Ross might well need a substantial amount of technical and quality assurance assistance and advice from Malston personnel. John Thomas was not sure whether his management colleagues would be as excited about this idea as he was.

Management Committee Meeting

John Thomas asked that bread flour be put on the agenda for the next management committee meeting. The president and all those reporting directly to him met once every two weeks to discuss matters of corporate interest. At the meeting, John explained what he was trying to do, making very clear that no commitments had been made of any kind. He explained he wished to pursue the alternative, but was unable to promise results. As John expected, the vice presidents of marketing and operations were both very concerned about the quality of the flour the Ross Mill might be able to produce. Both vice presidents felt that any drop in quality level of the finished product would affect sales adversely. The vice president of operations was highly skeptical about the Ross Mill's ability to meet Malston's high standards.

John Thomas did not try to minimize these concerns and agreed wholeheartedly that top-quality flour had to be produced for this venture to be feasible. He said:

> I cannot do it alone, I need your help to make sure that the quality will be acceptable. Do we have any people in our organization with the necessary expertise to help a new supplier like this? The last thing I'm interested in is bringing a supplier on stream who cannot meet our quality standards. The Ross brothers are highly capable individuals on soft wheat flour. Is it possible they may need help to get started on bread flour? Also, I'm sure that if we can assist Hellibell in getting the right kind of equipment in the first place and appropriate staff training support from the equipment vendor, that we are improving our chances of assuring high quality flour. Frankly, I believe you have identified our greatest risk in this venture. If we don't face up to it squarely, we may be stuck with high-cost flour for years to come. I think we can minimize our risk if we are willing to get involved more than we usually would with our normal suppliers. That's part of the price we have to pay. If you have staff in marketing, production, engineering, or anywhere else in the organization that can help us bring this venture to a satisfactory conclusion, we may be able to enjoy the rewards of it for years to come. Can we create a special interest group from which we can draw the appropriate resources when required?

The consensus of the management committee was that Malston should at least push it to the next steps to see if the project might be viable. John Thomas was encouraged to negotiate with Peter

Hellibell. He was expected to report on progress during the regular management committee meetings.

The Proposal to Hellibell

After the management committee meeting, John Thomas phoned Peter Hellibell to see if they could get together. They set a date in the following week. In the intervening period, John Thomas tried to think out how he might approach Hellibell. Hellibell appeared to be a straightforward type and John wondered if it might not be the best approach to be open about the benefits Malston expected to get out of any kind of a deal. He believed that the preliminary meeting would best be confined to Peter Hellibell and himself. If Hellibell expressed interest, it would be possible to bring in appropriate people later. If Hellibell was not interested, then the need for others might not exist.

When Peter Hellibell appeared at John Thomas' office at the appointed time, the two of them first engaged in the usual pleasantries. When John asked how Peter's plans were coming along, Peter responded that he would like to expand more quickly, but that ready cash was a problem. John said that he had an idea for more rapid expansion, and asked if Hellibell would be interested in hearing more about it.

John explained the difficulties Malston had been facing in trying to get truly competitive pricing for bread flour. He explained how he had visited all of the major mills in the area and how he had come to the conclusion that the mills were all overcharging and maintaining an artificially high price level.

> JOHN: It seems to me that this problem of ours might become an opportunity for you. You are interested in expanding your mill. We are interested in getting a bread flour supplier who is willing to supply a high-quality product at a reasonable price. We know from our earlier acquaintance with your organization that you can supply high-quality soft wheat flour. It is not a simple switch to acceptable bread flour but we think it can be done. Only if you can meet our quality standards is there any interest at all on our part to proceed. We don't want to run any risks that the flour you might be able to supply would not meet our standards. That's the risk you run. If you go out and commit yourself to equipment with much capacity, but cannot meet our standards, you're going to be in deep trouble. We're willing

to give you assistance if you need it to help you get the show on the road, but we want to make it very clear that the quality has to be tops and the price acceptable. Failure to meet either condition removes all of our interest. In my travels to the mills, I've come across the notion of using a cost-price formula. It seems to me that the notion of covering costs and allowing for a reasonable profit margin is the only way to go in this kind of venture. That means you must be willing to share your cost estimates with us and show us information you normally might not want to give to your customers. On the other hand, if you manage to accomplish all we require, there might be a good chunk of business in this for you and an opportunity to expand into an area which would normally be closed to you if we did not extend a helping hand.

PETER: Obviously, what you are talking about here is much bigger than anything to which I had given any thought. All of my thinking to date has been oriented toward the soft wheat flour market. I can see where there might be some advantages in this new idea for me, but I'm going to have to think it over very carefully. Let me come back to you in a couple of weeks when I have some facts and figures and we can talk more sensibly about this notion then. I'm hopeful that we can both get out of this what we really want.

In the subsequent weeks, Peter Hellibell and John Thomas were in regular contact, both face to face and by telephone. Both of them realized that it would take about a year before the Ross Mill could complete its expansion and install new equipment, even though much of the same equipment could be used for producing hard and soft wheat flour. Hellibell had met with his bankers and found them receptive to supplying expansion funds, provided a promise of Malston business could be obtained. John Thomas felt he could initially give 25 to 30 percent of his hard wheat flour requirements to the Ross Mill and increase it, if necessary, later. Various representatives from Malston's staff were called in to provide assistance in the areas of engineering, cost estimating, and quality control. Specific details were worked out on the disposal of the mill-feed by-products, the kinds of yields that could be expected, and how the flour would be transported since the Ross Mill didn't own a fleet of trucks.

Considerable discussion centered on choosing an appropriate profit margin. Peter Hellibell believed that the 3 percent margin proposed by John Thomas was not sufficient and wanted a 7 percent allowance instead. John Thomas made it clear that 7 percent was far too high and both parties eventually settled on a 4 percent figure. The cost-price formula agreed to by both sides is shown in Table 2–1.

Once Peter Hellibell and John Thomas agreed between themselves on the major aspects of the deal, they were ready to draw a formal contract. At this stage, legal advice on both sides was obtained. This resulted in a new set of negotiations as the lawyer on the Hellibell side tried to ensure certain guarantees for his client that John Thomas and Malston were not prepared to grant. One of the last stumbling blocks was Malston's insistence on having the right of first refusal if Hellibell decided to sell the mill. Eventually, some three months after the initial approach by John Thomas, all details were worked out to the satisfaction of both sides.

The Building

Between the time the contract was signed and the first load of flour was delivered, both firms had a great deal to do with respect to the mill expansion. Because the Ross Mill had no experience with milling bread flour, nor with the installation of new equipment and mill expansion, John Thomas kept in close contact with Hellibell during the initial year. He saw to it that Malston provided technical support to the Ross Mill as the expansion took place. As the start-up date for bread flour milling approached, experts from Malston worked with Ross Mill personnel to ensure that the equipment ran smoothly and that quality levels were reached. Therefore, it was not by luck that the first shipment was delivered on schedule and was of first-rate quality. Substantial planning and hard work by both firms made it possible.

Continued Performance

As the contract progressed, Malston technical people worked closely with Ross Mill people to keep good lines of communication open between the two firms. John also visited the mill on numerous occasions to reinforce his interest in the project's success. He also suggested that Hellibell hire a technical person and expand his quality-control lab to monitor the quality levels of all his prod-

TABLE 2-1 Pricing Formula

Cost of Wheat	Base Cost	Add Incoming Charges	Total Cost per Metric Ton	Cost per MT (metric ton)	
				Roll Flour	Bread Flour
A. Published price for domestic use				(40% 12½% protein) (60% 13½% protein)	(100% 12½% protein)
12½% Protein Wheat	$ 191.06 MT	$ 23.15	$ 214.21		
13½% Protein Wheat	$ 202.82 MT	$ 23.15	$ 225.97		
Cost of wheat used to mill 1 MT flour = 1.38 MT wheat.			$221.26 × 1.38 $214.21 × 1.38	$305.34	$295.61
B. Add Cost of Direct Labor				4.40	4.40
C. Add Cost of Overhead				19.18	19.18
D. Add Cost of Enrichment				1.10	1.10
E. Add for Profit (A + B + C + D) × 4%				13.20	12.81
F. Add Delivery Costs				4.19	4.19
Gross Selling Price per Metric Ton				$347.41	$337.29

Less Selling Price of .370 by-product feed
Established price of feed as published Wednesday of each week of preceding month:

	Bran (1 part)	Shorts (2 parts)	Average (1 bran/2 shorts)	Average for Month	Discount Allowed	Net Selling Price per MT		
1st week	147.70	177.08	167.28					
2nd week	147.70	178.96	168.54					
3rd week	147.70	178.96	168.54	164.17	3.09	161.08		
4th week	147.70	170.53	162.92			× .370		
5th week	147.70	156.47	153.55			59.60		
							59.60	59.60
Net Selling Price—Bulk FOB Bakery							$287.81	$277.69

47

ucts and provide a service representative to visit his customers. Hellibell agreed to these suggestions.

Once John Thomas was satisfied that the Ross Mill was meeting his quantity/quality objectives, he started the next round of negotiations with the existing vendors. He explained that unless they were willing to improve their prices, he would start reducing the quantities purchased. As the Ross Mill supplied larger and larger volumes of bread flour, John was able to reduce purchases substantially from those vendors who were unwilling to meet Malston's new price objectives. Thus, within a period of about six months, he was able to bring all of the remaining vendors to the Ross Mill price level. The combined savings from the Ross Mill and the regular vendors amounted to 7 percent per year, or $924,000. Thus, John Thomas found that he had successfully broken through the price barriers on bread flour.

As the three-year contract with the Ross Mill drew to a close, John Thomas wondered how to proceed next with the mill. Should another contract be drawn and for what length of time, or should the Ross Mill from here on in be treated like any other vendor?

REVERSE MARKETING LESSONS
FROM MALSTON BAKERY

This typical example of a reverse marketing effort will be used to identify the chronological steps in the reverse marketing process. It can be seen that John Thomas and Peter Hellibell and their respective organizations passed through distinctly different phases as the reverse marketing progressed. The analysis of interest here will be these phases and not so much the economic implications, which will be discussed in the next chapter.

A total of eleven phases can be identified in the reverse marketing process. These are:

Phase	*Purpose*
1. Fundamental research	Assess general need and potential
2. Specific research	Identify specific requirements and target vendors

3. Key decision point	Decide whether or not to use reverse marketing.
4. Design	Determine objectives, strategies, and plan
5. Organizational support	Obtain internal acceptance for design
6. Design review	Review and prepare management team
7. Negotiation	Put proposal to vendor
8. Agreement in principle	Make deal verbally
9. Written agreement	Put deal in writing
10. Contract administration	Make the agreement work
11. Reverse marketing options	Terminate or change the reverse marketing agreement

Although not all of these phases may be present in every reverse marketing effort, an understanding of the complete set is useful. The following discussion will therefore cover each of these phases in detail, with appropriate reference to the Malston Bakery case.

PHASE 1: FUNDAMENTAL RESEARCH

The fundamental research phase is the starting point for reverse marketing. It elicits areas of potential by examining the present situation and future scenarios with respect to quality, quantity, delivery, price, service, and other criteria.* For each of these criteria an assessment must be made of the firm's current situation—in effect a current status report of its satisfaction with respect to these criteria. For example, taking a specific commodity or requirement (such as bread flour in the Malston case), the purchaser must consider the following questions: What are the current quality, quantity, delivery, price, service, and other criteria for this requirement? Next an assessment of these same factors with respect to the current market situation should be made.

---

*Other criteria may include special terms and conditions, warranties, special delivery or stocking arrangements, access to R & D information, warning of impending price changes, and flexibility to change requirements.

These same fundamental supply criteria must next be examined for the future—assessing both the user firm's future requirements and the projected future status of the market. In the Malston Bakery case, John Thomas considered that a major part of his role as Director of Purchases was to do precisely this—to monitor the current and future needs of the major items used by Malston to seek better value for the firm. He did this as an ongoing function so that all of the major purchases at Malston would come under regular scrutiny.

It should be kept in mind that the future time frames may well differ depending upon the requirement in question. For example, a major purchaser of strawberries may have a three-year time horizon whereas for a major purchaser of a raw material or an energy source the time horizon may be 10 to 30 years (or even longer). The opportunity to engage in reverse marketing will vary depending upon the lead time available. With very short lead times reverse marketing may be very difficult, if not impossible. A long lead time often allows latitude for reverse marketing options. In the Malston Bakery case, some of the items scrutinized by John Thomas would have a relatively short lead time, such as office supplies and word processing equipment, while others would have a much longer lead time, such as new raw material sources.

Figure 2–1 sets out four information frames in the reverse marketing decision; showing the requirements and the market, both in the current and future time frames. Each of these four quadrants is broken down into the purchasing criteria of quality, quantity, delivery, price, service, and other.

Figure 2–2 shows the five most important analyses or "matches" that arise from these four information frames. The first or "Match 1" lines up current needs with the current market. The matching of current and future requirements is labeled "Match 2." Current market versus future market is "Match 3." Future requirements versus future markets creates "Match 4." In "Match 5" all four quadrants are compared simultaneously. This simultaneous comparison should provide an overall view of current and future supply positions relative to that of the market. Match 5 is the key match as it forces examination of the possible combinations of requirements and markets. In the Malston case, John Thomas, as part of his ongoing program to seek better value for the firm in the items for which he was responsible, was continually thinking about these five matches. It was during this match-

FIGURE 2–1.
The Four Information Frames Pertinent to the Fundamental
Research Phase in Reverse Marketing

	REQUIREMENTS	THE MARKET
CURRENT	Current requirements of the organization with respect to: — Quality — Quantity — Delivery — Price — Service — Other	Current market performance or capability with respect to: — Quality — Quantity — Delivery — Price — Service — Other
FUTURE	Future expected requirements of the organization with respect to: — Quality — Quantity — Delivery — Price — Service — Other	Future expected market performance or capability with respect to: — Quality — Quantity — Delivery — Price — Service — Other

FIGURE 2–2.
The Five Most Common Matches Between Requirements and Markets

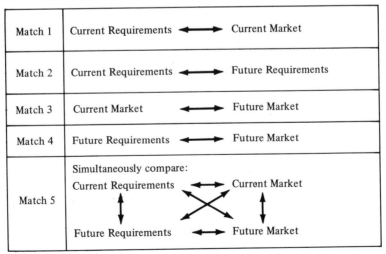

Match 1	Current Requirements ⟷ Current Market
Match 2	Current Requirements ⟷ Future Requirements
Match 3	Current Market ⟷ Future Market
Match 4	Future Requirements ⟷ Future Market
Match 5	Simultaneously compare: Current Requirements ⟷ Current Market Future Requirements ⟷ Future Market

ing process that he realized that his bread flour suppliers were continually increasing their prices and would likely continue to do so in the future. Price was the key concern, even though during his matching exercise the other value criteria of quality, quantity, delivery, service, and other were quite acceptable, both for the present and for the foreseeable future.

Having come to the conclusion that price was unacceptable as a part of matches 1, 2, and 4 and that market conditions were unlikely to change as a result of matches 3 and 5, John Thomas came to the conclusion that it would require unusual action on his part to alter market conditions. By developing a new supplier willing to provide quality bread flour at lower than market prices, he was able to alter future market conditions significantly.

It was not a simple task, however, and the idea of reverse marketing did not at first occur to John Thomas. He engaged in a substantial amount of data gathering, both within his own organization to determine current and future requirements, and also in the market to determine current and future supply conditions.

A Second Example of the Matching Process: The Metalan Case

This fundamental research phase and its implications are so important that a second example is in order. Figure 2-3 shows some key information about the Metalan Corporation's requirement for PR 179, a catalyst currently used only in its laboratory. This item

FIGURE 2-3.
Key Information About a Second Example (The Metalan Corporation's Requirement for PR 179)

	REQUIREMENTS	THE MARKET
CURRENT	Quantity — very low (C item) Price — reasonable, of no great concern	Quantity — plentiful supply — buyer's market Price — relatively low — buyer's market
FUTURE	Quantity — very high (A item) Price — of major concern	Quantity — questionable — seller's market Price — high — seller's market

currently has a very low annual requirement; it is a "C" item in a current market of plentiful supply. Future anticipated requirements are, however, very high because of plans to use PR 179 in a new production process. Moreover, future market conditions are expected to be tight. Apparently, quality, service, and other criteria are not of overriding concern in this situation. Match 1 of current requirements versus current market shows an item of low priority. As a "C" item, primary concern should probably be to ensure availability without wasting procurement time and effort on it. This could be accomplished by buying it along with a number of other small items, possibly as part of a systems contract or a blanket order. It might well be acquired from a local wholesaler or distributor. Price would not be a matter of concern. Match 2 of current versus future requirements shows a drastic increase in consumption, however. Thus, the item changes from a "C" to an "A" category. It will therefore require special management attention. Match 3 of current versus future market shows a tightening of the market. Match 4 of future high requirements with an expected tight future market should start ringing a number of warning bells. First and foremost, availability (or a combination of quantity and delivery) will be of concern. Second, it will be difficult to obtain a good price under tough market conditions. The fifth match—simultaneously considering current and future requirements and markets—now permits consideration of specific procurement strategies. Obviously, continuing to buy in the current manner makes no sense for the future. Perhaps the item could be made in-house, perhaps a long-term contract with a manufacturer is in order, perhaps reverse marketing is an option. Please note, however, that action may have to be started now and quickly to avoid serious supply problems in the future. If the tight market develops too quickly, it may be difficult to satisfy simultaneously both procurement objectives of availability and acceptable price.

What makes this example particularly interesting is the current situation. Normally, it would be unusual to pay any particular procurement attention to a "C" item in plentiful supply. The example, nevertheless, underscores the need to go beyond the current situation and to predict future requirements and future markets to obtain a complete picture.

This example further underscores the need to include procurement personnel on long-range planning task forces, new product development groups, and any other activities of the organization which may affect future supply needs. Most supply groups are under continuing daily pressure to supply current requirements. It is often difficult to find the time and resources to examine future requirements and markets when current supply problems cry for attention. It was precisely for this reason that Harold E. Fearon[1] suggested the formation of a purchasing research activity person or group to ensure that the study of future requirements and markets would be carried out.

A Variation in the Metalan Example

The Metalan example may be discussed a bit further. Given a specific set of data, at least three quite different procurement strategies presented themselves. Had market conditions been different, such as tight supply currently and an expected future buyers' market, a totally different procurement action would be called for. Even though all three alternatives—(1) making in house, (2) buying directly from a manufacturer under long-term contract, and (3) developing a supplier—may still be considered serious options, the timing of these options might be substantially different, particularly with the second option. Also, the future concern now centers primarily on price, since availability is not expected to be so difficult in a buyers' market.

Both the Malston and Metalan examples have used only some of the six purchasing criteria. The same exercise with the five matches should obviously be done with all criteria of quality, quantity, delivery, price, service, and other, to assess whether reverse marketing would be appropriate for the particular requirement.

It would be unusual if, after such a matching exercise, concern centered on all criteria. It would be more normal to find concern with one or a few criteria, such as was the case at Malston or Metalan. For some organizations improvement of quality may be of primary concern, for others it could be price, for others domestic content, technology, or minority sourcing, to name just a few. In later chapters, these differing objectives will be examined more closely as they impact on the reverse marketing process.

It is clear that the activities engaged in during the fundamental research phase should be carried out in any well-managed procurement organization whether it engages in reverse marketing or not. It will be assumed from here on that reverse marketing will be considered a serious option and the remaining phases will be described accordingly.

PHASE 2: SPECIFIC RESEARCH

The purpose of both the fundamental research and specific research phases is to determine whether engaging in reverse marketing could present opportunities for the organization. The fundamental research of phase 1 has elicited those broad areas where reverse marketing is a possibility. Specific research examines promising options in more detail. In the specific research phase the focus is on a particular commodity, classification of parts, and on specific vendors.

For example, in the Malston case specific types of bread flour were identified as well as one specific reverse marketing option. It was interesting, but not unusual, that the Ross Mill was already one of Malston's suppliers for other flour products. Reverse marketing does not have to involve only suppliers with which no prior business relationship existed. There are many advantages in dealing with existing vendors, as the perceived risk of failure is lower and the need for developing new relationships from scratch disappears.

In specific research, detailed requirements information is collected on all six procurement criteria for the specific commodity. At the same time, detailed information is gathered about the potential vendor, including managerial, financial, production, and technological strengths and weaknesses. Again, as in the case of fundamental research, this type of data gathering is in itself not unusual. Much of it would normally be done in any case involving a serious supply evaluation. What makes it special is the objective of engaging in reverse marketing. What is it about this specific requirement and this specific vendor that will make a successful pitch possible? Knowing that a proposal will have to be forthcoming results in high-quality research that is probably more thorough than that done in response to a typical marketing initiative from a vendor. For the case of Malston Bakery, John Thomas carried out some specific research simultaneously with his fundamental research. In examining the milling process for flour, he came to the conclusion that existing suppliers were able to extract too high a price. He also obtained the idea of a formula approach. Later, when faced with the Ross Mill possibility, he determined that the new owner had only limited financial resources, an important piece of information in the formulation of the subsequent pitch.

It is likely that many of the value analyses or value engineering techniques will be useful during the specific research phase. These will help to identify specific areas of value improvement and provide ideas for concrete action both in the areas of design and specifications as well as specific vendor alternatives. Training of procurement personnel in value analysis/engineering techniques is probably essential in effective reverse marketing.

Both the fundamental and specific research phases are intended to be periods of information gathering. The boundary line between them may be fuzzy and it is not necessary to see these two activities as mutually exclusive. Chronologically, it makes sense to leave investigation of specific commodity subgroups or specific vendors toward the end of the information gathering phase. For example, it is probably desirable to look at all metal castings first, before considering aluminum castings, or within aluminum castings, those under or over a specific weight or size range. Similarly, it seems reasonable to examine total market conditions before concerning oneself with specific players in that market.

On the assumption that the information gathering is now complete (a convenient but probably unrealistic assumption), the next step in this phase is to assess the options.

Assessing the Options

In theory the purchaser should be able to assess the various supply options by using reasoned judgment and by placing the probability of success along with the payoff for each option. For example, options could include: (1) continuing the relationship with the same supplier, (2) switching vendors, (3) making the item in-house, and (4) engaging in reverse marketing. To assess the reverse marketing option it might be very difficult for some people to make a reasonable estimate of the probable outcome. To alleviate this it may be necessary actually to engage in the reverse marketing exercise up to the point where negotiations with the potential supplier have been completed. This may be necessary to obtain the needed data in order to make a comparison among the various supply options that are open. John Thomas in the Malston case had assessed and followed up on some of the options open to him in his attempt to lower the price of bread flour. The most obvious option, that of talking with his current suppliers and getting them to reduce prices, proved futile. Since Malston's current suppliers consisted of all of those in the industry that milled bread flour, the option did not exist to approach bread flour millers that were currently not suppliers. The option of buying a source of supply had been addressed in the firm's consideration of the purchase of the Ross Mill, but this had been rejected by the board of directors. When none of the above alternatives proved feasible, John Thomas set out to find out more about the milling business, and this is where his visits to all of his current suppliers proved invaluable. During his visits to the mills he learned of the flour cost and pricing structure and became convinced that indeed the price increases to which Malston was being subjected were excessive. This realization led to the conclusion that the only alternative left to be explored was that of Malston developing its own source of supply for bread flour. Even when development of the Ross Mill emerged as a possible option, it was necessary to conduct extensive negotiations with Peter Hellibell to determine if this really was a viable option.

If, upon comparison of the various supply options, the reverse marketing option emerges as the most desirable one, the strategy that is then developed will include a reverse marketing plan. On

FIGURE 2–4.
Specific Research Sequence

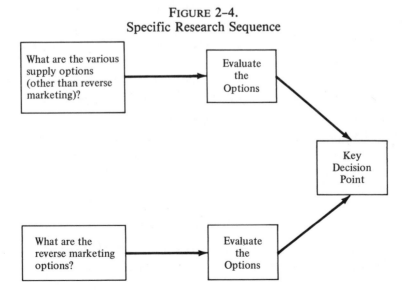

the other hand, if no reverse marketing opportunities appear feasible, the implication is that the existing methods of supply or options are functioning as well as can be expected. The formal decision whether to engage in reverse marketing or not has been left to the next phase. Figure 2–4 illustrates the sequence of the specific research phase.

PHASE 3: KEY DECISION POINT

The key decision is "Should reverse marketing be engaged in or should the conventional sourcing be continued?"

In determining whether reverse marketing is worth pursuing, there has to be a decision rule such as "the reverse marketing option must result in this specific improvement to be considered viable." In the Malston Bakery case, John Thomas felt that a minimum of 7 percent saving on the flour costs would be necessary for his project to be considered worthwhile. Also, the probabilities of success and failure must be weighed. The potential payoff in case of success could be improvements in quality, quantity, delivery, price, service, and other considerations. The costs to the organization if the project failed could be measured in terms of the time spent and actual costs incurred in the unsuccessful reverse marketing attempt. These same types of costs may also be faced by the potential supplier organization. John Thomas of Malston Bakery realized at the outset that there would be no guarantee of success in the development of the Ross Mill as a new source of supply for bread flour. Failure would have its costs, both for Malston and for the Ross Mill.

Before the key decision to engage in reverse marketing is made, all the possible options must be evaluated, including:

1. Should one source be utilized or more than one?
2. Should local or nonlocal suppliers be used?
3. Should a small, a medium-sized, or a large supplier be used?
4. Should a standard or custom-made item be used?
5. Should the organization buy outside or make the item within?
6. Should the item be redesigned or kept as it is?

Although other options may be available depending upon the circumstances, the point is that all possible options should be assessed before making the key decision of whether or not to engage in reverse marketing. At the key decision point, if the decision is made not to engage in reverse marketing the implication is that the organization is satisfied with its current sources of supply. However, if the decision is made to go with the reverse marketing option, there are two possible reasons behind the decision:

1. All supply options have been evaluated and the reverse marketing option is the only feasible option. This means that all the reverse marketing phases will be gone through:

1. Fundamental research	7. Negotiation
2. Specific research	8. Agreement in principle
3. Key decision point	9. Written agreement
4. Design	10. Contract administration
5. Organizational support	11. Reverse marketing
6. Design review	options

Presumably, in the case of failure, the process will be repeated until successful.

2. Reverse marketing will be engaged in provided it meets certain decision rules, but the organization will still have conventional supply options to fall back on if the reverse marketing exercise proves unsuccessful. If the reverse marketing operation goes according to plan, then all of the phases listed above will be covered. The Malston Bakery example falls into this category because John Thomas still had his conventional sources of bread flour to fall back on if the Ross Mill project proved unsuccessful.

This second option required reverse marketing to be engaged in to obtain enough data to determine whether the reverse marketing route is a viable option. In this case the reverse marketing exercise will have to include at least the first four phases—that is, fundamental research, specific research, key decision point, and design—and possibly also organizational support, design review, and negotiation. Figure 2-5 lays out the key decision point phase in more detail.

It is useful to see reverse marketing as a specific option to be considered with both its costs and opportunities. To assume that it will automatically result in a roaring success is to deceive oneself. The possibility of failure and its consequences must be part

FIGURE 2–5.
Key Decision Point

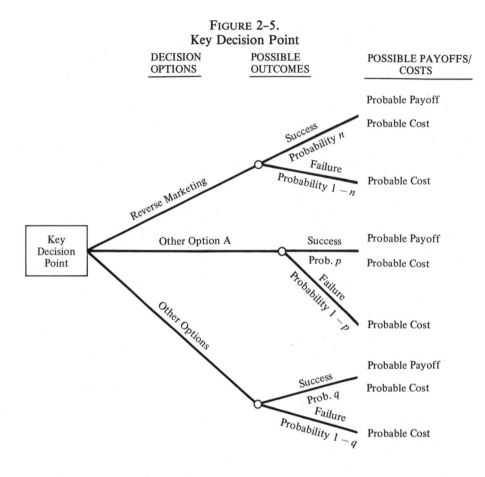

of the decision as well. For the remainder of this chapter, the assumption will be that the decision has been to engage in reverse marketing in all its phases right to a successful conclusion.

PHASE 4: DESIGN

The design phase should set out a plan for the whole supplier development project. The starting point should be a review of the steps completed to date, namely the fundamental research, specific research, and key decision point phases. In doing this the purchaser can summarize and reassess the rationale used in these first three phases in light of an overall plan. Also this review exercise may uncover other options and may reveal that more data needs to be gathered, or objectives revised. Next, an analysis of the logic that underlies the plan should be undertaken. This should lead to the justification of the plan itself and include the identification of the firm's position of strength with respect to its potential suppliers. Position of strength is a relative concept and it enables the purchaser to set objectives and achieve them. The stronger the position of strength the more demanding the reverse marketing objectives can be. What, then, gives a party a position of strength in the reverse marketing context? Answers to the following questions will shed some light on the question: Who needs whom more? Who will suffer more if no agreement is reached? Who will gain the most if agreement is reached?

Listed below are some factors that can lead to a position of strength for the parties involved in reverse marketing.

Factors Leading to Positions of Strength

Factors Giving Purchaser a Position of Strength	*Factors Giving Potential Supplier a Position of Strength*
—the only purchaser of the item	—the only supplier of the requirement
—careful homework	—careful homework
—seen in the marketplace as an attractive firm to deal with	—a particularly good reputation
—general market conditions favor buyers	—general market conditions favor sellers
—knowledge that the supplier needs the business badly, e.g. has excess capacity or is holding large inventories	—knowledge that the purchaser shows preference for brands or technology offered
—many potential suppliers exist	—many potential purchasers exist
—plenty of lead time	—purchaser short of lead time
—a large volume which represents a large part of supplier's capacity	—purchaser's volume is insignificant
—taking the initiative	—taking the initiative

The assessment of position of strength of both parties requires judgment and any individual factor may be seen as more important by one person than another. Also the weighing of one position versus the other may result in different conclusions, depending upon who is making the assessment.

In the Malston Bakery case it appears that each party holds a roughly equal position of strength. Malston Bakery needs an alternate source of supply and the Ross Mill needs the bread flour contract from Malston to facilitate its mill expansion. Neither party can accomplish its objectives without the other, yet both can survive well without the other.

Keeping in mind the earlier tentative objectives, the alternatives under consideration, and the relative position of strength of both parties, more specific reverse marketing objectives should now be set.

The analysis of the position of strength of each party in reverse marketing leads to the identification of reasonable objectives. There is no point in the purchaser's setting arbitrarily ambitious objectives. This is likely to lead to frustration for both parties and an unsuccessful development effort. In the Malston case the original focus was on a price objective of 7 percent improvement. Later, additional objectives of quality (a major concern to both marketing and production personnel), quantity, and delivery were added.

Once the objectives of the reverse marketing plan are clearly stated, the steps that will have to be followed to accomplish these objectives must be carefully formulated. These steps include the organizational support, design review, negotiation, and agreement in principle phases with the rationale proper to each phase. The implementation steps determine who will do what. In the Malston case, John Thomas was involved in most activities, but a significant number of other people at Malston played an active role in the execution of the reverse marketing effort. It was obvious that Peter Hellibell would be the prime supplier contact. Sometimes, particularly in the case of a large vendor with whom no prior business relations exist, the best person to contact may not be obvious. How the pitch will be made needs to be carefully planned. What objections are likely to be raised by the other party and how can these be overcome? Fortunately, the earlier homework and especially the analysis of position of strength of both parties will be helpful. For example, in the Malston case, John Thomas knew that Peter Hellibell was anxious to expand but lacked financial resources. Thus, a plan that allowed Peter to expand and John to achieve his price objective found mutual benefit for both parties. It was this realization that formed the heart of the Malston argument.

A substantial number of actual reverse marketing examples will be given in this text. These will illustrate the actual plans and efforts used by various purchasers in a variety of settings. It is obvious that a sound plan must be at the core of any successful effort. Presumably, with a complete plan the remaining steps in the reverse marketing effort are almost anticlimactic. They represent simply execution of what was intended and what made good business sense. In practice, it is seldom quite that simple.

In the Malston Bakery case, John Thomas did not have on paper a formal design for the whole project he envisioned, but he knew the final goal he wanted to achieve and the steps that would have to be covered to achieve that goal. It is suggested that committing the design of the reverse marketing project to paper is most useful.

In conclusion, the design phase provides the reverse marketing

FIGURE 2–6.
Steps in the Design Phase

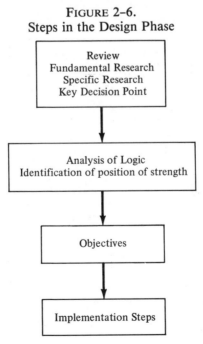

plan. It identifies the objectives and how they are to be achieved. (Figure 2–6 summarizes the main steps in the design phase.) This phase is the most important one in the process. It provides the logic for all that follows. A sound design cuts down on the elements of chance and luck and changes the activity from an improvisation to a carefully planned project.

PHASE 5: ORGANIZATIONAL SUPPORT

Very often one of the most difficult barriers in a reverse marketing plan is to overcome resistance within one's own organization. The more unusual the approach, the greater the internal resistance is likely to be. Listed below are some ideas that may assist in obtaining initial support and in overcoming internal resistance. Because a reverse marketing project often necessitates a change inside the purchaser's organization, the area of effecting organizational change is first addressed.

Effecting Change in One's Own Organization

A reverse marketing project often results in a marked departure from the traditional way in which the organization has dealt with its sourcing problems. To achieve success in obtaining organizational support, the purchaser should be aware of the principles of effecting change in organizations. Lippitt[2] stresses the importance of the person trying to introduce change in an organization by pointing out that their behavior often erects an impenetrable barrier between themselves and those who will be affected by the change. Changes in the organization that are necessitated by the reverse marketing project can take place in four different areas[3]:

1. *Knowledge.* There must be a generalization about the change experience itself. For example, in the Malston case, the president, Bill Simmons, was fully aware of the upward pressure on the price of bread flour by its suppliers and the other members of the management team were made cognizant of this via the management committee meetings.
2. *Skill.* Often new or modified skills are required. Again, in the Malston case, undertaking the reverse marketing project would require very close cooperation between Malston's technical people and people at the Ross Mill, with Malston

personnel providing a teaching role to the supplier—a new activity for them.

3. *Attitude.* New feelings are aroused through experiencing success with them. Both the Malston vice presidents of marketing and production were skeptical that the Ross Mill could produce bread flour of a quality level which would meet that of the current suppliers. To gain their support, their current attitudes would have to be changed.

4. *Values.* Often values and beliefs need alteration. All members of the top management team at Malston believed that the market could be relied upon to provide the best possible prices. Confronting reality is the first aspect of a model of planned change—so that all the known implications of the change can be thought through before the plan is introduced.

If the plan cannot gain internal support as it is, then change or modification is needed.

Obtaining organizational support was crucial for John Thomas. Without it his plan was doomed to fail. In presenting his plan to the key management committee, acknowledging individual members' concerns about the project, and stressing that by working as a team the whole organization would benefit, he was able to gain their confidence. If he had not handled this step properly, his plan could possibly have met insurmountable internal resistance from key management people at each stage of the project.

John Thomas started his discussion on reducing flour costs with the president, Bill Simmons. He then proceeded to win over members of the management committee by pointing out the benefits to Malston in developing the Ross Mill and acknowledging that their quality level concerns were very real ones indeed. He then promised (and followed through) to keep the management committee informed of progress in the plan and above all he had the trust and confidence of the committee before he formally went ahead with his plan.

PHASE 6: DESIGN REVIEW

In this phase the person actually in charge of the supplier contact phase of the project should review the plan of action to ensure that each person understands his or her role in the following phases. It is important that the persons involved are brought up to date on any recent developments that can affect the project. It may become apparent that certain key information is still missing or that someone else must be sold internally before the plan can go formally outside the firm. Once this is done, the group should revise the design as necessary, given its objectives and any changes in circumstances that have arisen since the plan was first formulated. This phase also serves as a preparation and a rehearsal for the negotiation phase with the potential supplier. Questions such as "Does everyone who is involved in the negotiation process know what they are to do?" should be addressed. This is an important phase as it is the putting into words the plan which has been worked out and agreed to by the key participants.

It is not too late at this stage to improve upon the plan. Any significant adjustments at this point may have to be referred back to others for approval before being formally incorporated into the plan. The design review phase may be thought of as a rehearsal, review, and a last quality check of the plan before supplier contact is initiated.

Since John Thomas of Malston Bakery was undertaking most of the Ross Mill negotiations himself, the design review and rehearsal phase could be done by himself without having to coordinate others. He had, of course, cleared the principal phases of the plan with the management committee. In his preparation for the initial negotiations with Peter Hellibell he felt that a one-on-one meeting would be the most productive, with others to be brought into the negotiations later if needed.

PHASE 7: NEGOTIATION

The negotiation phase deals with putting the proposal across to the vendor. It is the actual contact with supplier personnel to present the advantages of the deal. It is already obvious that the proposal is of interest to the purchaser. Unless there are benefits to the supplier as well, it is unlikely that the vendor will be keen to cooperate. Unless there is mutual benefit, reverse marketing is unlikely to go far. In negotiation terms, it must be a win-win type of negotiation.

The nature of the arguments to be used and the way these are to be presented, by whom, to whom, when, and where should, of course, all have been decided during the design phase.

John Thomas in the Malston case had carefully laid down plans for his negotiations with Peter Hellibell of the Ross Mill. He began by having an informal one-on-one meeting with Hellibell, so as not to intimidate him with many "experts" present. He explained clearly Malston's current position with respect to bread flour, the options he faced, and what he had done to date and how. Malston's dilemma presented an opportunity for Hellibell. The negotiation phase with Hellibell extended over a three-month period as data had to be obtained and discussed by both parties. There was give and take by both parties on such issues as the profit margin initially requested by Hellibell.

What makes reverse marketing unique is that the initiative for the proposal rests with the purchaser; it forces the purchaser to do careful homework, perhaps examining requirements more carefully than might otherwise be done. The better definition of purchaser needs may potentially reap benefits similar to those obtained by a careful review of function in value analysis/engineering. Taking the initiative also makes it possible for the negotiation phase to center on the purchaser's proposal.

The process during this phase is essentially that of any negotiation. Compared to the traditional buying and selling context, the key difference is that in reverse marketing the selling of the proposal is done by the purchasing side. How this is actually accomplished will be shown in many examples in addition to the Malston case.

PHASE 8: AGREEMENT IN PRINCIPLE

At some point in the negotiation with the potential supplier, it will be realized that the two organizations can work together for mutual benefit and that a deal is possible. At this stage not all the points in the plan will have been settled, but the important ones will have been—the ones that can make or break the deal. In the Malston case this point was reached fairly early in the negotiation phase when both John Thomas and Peter Hellibell realized that the plan was mutually beneficial.

The agreement in principle phase signals that a deal has been struck. Whereas prior to this phase it is possible (and not at all unusual) to return to earlier phases in the process, once the deal has been agreed to, this will no longer be possible. For example, during the negotiation phase the vendor may say: "I know that a German firm intends to set up shop here in town, but that should not change anything." If the purchaser was unaware of this new entry into the market, and if it could affect the plan, it is not at all too late to break off negotiations and do some further specific research on this new lead.

This movement from phase to phase, backwards and forwards, is more realistic than the simple progression identified so far. While the purchaser is engaged in fundamental and specific research, some organizational support and preliminary negotiation may actually be carried out. While the design is worked on, the need for further information becomes apparent. This process of skipping through the phases in the reverse marketing process is illustrated in Figure 2-7.

However, once phase 8 has been reached, it is no longer possible to move backwards in the process. It is important, therefore, to be certain that the deal does make sense before tying the knot. Even though, theoretically, it might be possible to pull out after agreement in principle has been reached, it would not be common, and might be interpreted as bargaining in bad faith. Particularly if the purchaser wishes to pull out after originating the idea in the first place, this might seem very strange.

It is wise at this point to sit down and recap with the potential supplier just what has been agreed upon.

At each phase in the process, adequate records must be kept with copies to those who should be kept informed. It is very important to record any verbal agreement.

There is probably no better time than right after the verbal agreement has been reached to review what actually was accomplished, both in objectives and process. The assessment of the process to date should be a learning experience which may be used in subsequent reverse marketing efforts. The review should ask the following types of questions: (1) Are we achieving our objectives? (2) Was our research adequate? (3) Was our design good? (4) Was our organizational support sound? (5) Was our design review appropriate? (6) Did the team members perform to expectations? and (7) What could have been improved at any point before or during the negotiations with the supplier? Such question-

FIGURE 2-7.
Possible Looping Options in the Reverse Marketing Process

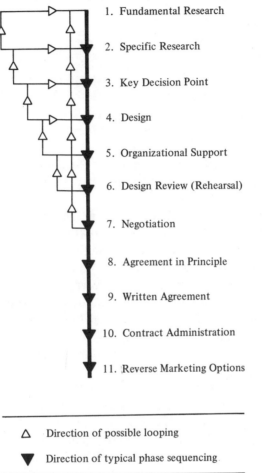

1. Fundamental Research

2. Specific Research

3. Key Decision Point

4. Design

5. Organizational Support

6. Design Review (Rehearsal)

7. Negotiation

8. Agreement in Principle

9. Written Agreement

10. Contract Administration

11. Reverse Marketing Options

△   Direction of possible looping

▼   Direction of typical phase sequencing

The above diagram illustrates that up to and including the Negotiation phase it is possible to go back (to loop) and revise any or all of the preceding phases. However, once Agreement in Principle has been reached, it is possible only to proceed forward through phases 9, 10, and 11, and not loop backward.

ing can lead to the avoidance of future mistakes and a steadily growing confidence in the ability to move through the various phases of the process.

The assumption at the conclusion of the agreement in principle phase is that all key points have been agreed to and documented in a letter to the supplier and that no subsequent changes will upset the agreement.

PHASE 9: WRITTEN AGREEMENT

The purchaser can maintain initiative and control after obtaining written agreement in principle from the supplier (phase 8) by drafting the contract. It is much easier to discuss the points in a contract from one's own work than from that of the supplier.

The contract should reflect the spirit of the verbal agreement. Since the possibility always exists that the contract may end up in court, clarity of language and completeness of details are vital to avoid later misunderstanding.

It is wise to try to cover all the normal eventualities at contract negotiation time, rather than leave matters to be resolved on an ad hoc basis as they arise. Even though it may be unpleasant to discuss potential problems when everyone has high expectations, possible eventualities should be covered in the contract. Tact should be used in bringing up future potential problems with the agreement as this can cause tension at this time.

From a purchasing standpoint, it is wise not to commit the firm to any long-term contract that the purchaser honestly does not believe it is possible to live with.

This written agreement phase can itself be a substantial negotiation between the parties. In the Malston case, the written agreement was prepared by the lawyers for both parties with substantial input by John Thomas and Peter Hellibell. This written agreement stage precipitated negotiations as contentious points were put in writing. For example, the issue of first right of refusal, should Peter Hellibell wish to sell the Ross Mill, became a point of serious concern.

PHASE 10: CONTRACT ADMINISTRATION

In effective reverse marketing, it is not good enough just to establish the contract, get it signed, and then forget about it. Since the true development of a supplier is an ongoing process, it is crucial to maintain the relationship effectively. It is essential that the supplier knows of the purchaser's difficulties and vice versa. The process must receive proper attention, which means adequate follow-up, consultation, and reminders.

It is during the run of the contract that both the purchaser's and supplier's true colors emerge. While it is necessary to monitor the supplier's performance, it is essential to verify that the purchaser's requests are realistic as the project progresses. With new suppliers there is often an initial break-in period during which both sides try to match systems, procedures, and expectations.

All of the normal purchasing rules regarding contract administration hold in this phase. It is purchasing's responsibility to set up lines of communication in advance so that early contract administration difficulties can be quickly resolved. Back-up capabilities should also be addressed in advance to prevent small problems from becoming large ones. In the Malston case John Thomas maintained close contact with Peter Hellibell of the Ross Mill during the initial stages of the contract. By developing and maintaining good communication links potential start-up problems were avoided.

Awareness of supplier inexperience with the project is important since this puts extra pressure on contract administration. John Thomas of Malston Bakery was cognizant that Ross Mill personnel were new to milling bread flour and so Malston provided extensive technical support during the machinery installation and preproduction period.

Monitoring the first deliveries under the new contract is also essential. Because of the special circumstances in reverse marketing, patience and encouragement should be demonstrated by the purchaser at this point. In the case of Malston Bakery, because of the close working relationship between Malston and Ross Mill personnel, it was not surprising that the quality level of the first delivery of bread flour was first rate. In some industries, such as the electronics field, it may take a number of years before a supplier reaches a fully acceptable quality status.

PHASE 11: REVERSE MARKETING OPTIONS

At the end of the first contract with the supplier, a decision point is reached. Should the reverse marketing be continued or a different relationship be established? The decision hinges on the issue as to when the supplier may be considered to be fully weaned.

In the Malston Bakery case, once the first three-year contract with the Ross Mill was completed and his other bread flour suppliers had come into line with their prices, John Thomas had to decide whether to treat the Ross Mill the same as all other suppliers. This might prove difficult considering all that the two firms had gone through together.

Some of the issues that enter into this decision are: (1) the size of the supplier. Is that firm able to operate successfully without further purchasing assistance? (2) How much investment has the purchaser made in the supplier? (3) What was the nature of the commitment made at the outset? Was it a long-term commitment or a short-term one? (4) What is the future need for products or services this supplier can provide?

Once a supplier has been developed to the point where it can successfully function without purchaser assistance, the purchaser must decide whether dealings with other suppliers will be influenced by the special relationship with the developed supplier. Potential suppliers may perceive the developed supplier as occupying a favored position. This issue is far more complex than it may seem at first glance. Some purchasers believe that reverse marketing never ends and that a special relationship and favored position are entirely appropriate. Others, and particularly those in public procurement feel that such a special relationship interferes with the competitive process and that the reverse marketing effort should be terminated as soon as possible.

In the Malston case John Thomas himself was not clear at what point the reverse marketing effort terminated and a regular purchaser-supplier relationship had started. Since flour was a repetitive and continuing requirement, the need for a continued supplier relationship was obvious, anyway. And because Peter Hellibell had already disclosed his full investment and cost position earlier, the Ross Mill occupied a position substantially different from the other traditional sources.

Nevertheless, it is during this final phase of reverse marketing options that the decision to terminate the relationship completely should at least be considered. On a one-time purchase, termination may be the only option open. It is also possible that the developed supplier may wish to terminate the business. It would probably be normal, however, to discuss termination reasons (and other options as well) carefully with the other party before severing the relationship.

BRIEF SUMMARY

1. Reverse marketing is a process with 11 phases:

Phase	*Purpose*
1. Fundamental research	— Assess general need and potential.
2. Specific research	— Identify specific requirements and target vendors.
3. Key decision point	— Use reverse marketing? Yes or No.
4. Design	— Determine objectives and strategies and plan.
5. Organizational support	— Obtain internal acceptance for design.
6. Design review	— Review and team preparation.
7. Negotiation	— Put proposal to vendor.
8. Agreement in principle	— Make deal verbally.
9. Written agreement	— Put deal in writing.
10. Contract administration	— Make the agreement work.
11. Reverse marketing options	— Terminate or change the reverse marketing agreement

2. The first seven phases (up to and including negotiation) probably overlap and loop in reality.
3. Successful reverse marketing depends on the effective management of this eleven phase process.

CHAPTER 3

Value and Price

In this chapter the emphasis is on value and price. Even though price is but one component of value, there are many procurement situations where price is a dominant concern.

The key objective for procurement is to obtain value for the money spent. The term "value" connotes utility or worth for an item and sometimes has no direct relationship to cost. However, typically the value of any service, material, or product is established by the minimum cost of other available alternatives that will perform the same functions. Value is a relative term, which may be categorized as value of use, of cost, of esteem, or of exchange.

Value is a concept that combines the procurement objectives of quality, quantity, delivery, price, service, and other under one umbrella. It therefore requires the exercise of judgment and is always concerned with trade-offs. Determining what constitutes good value is the responsibility of procurement personnel, aided by the expertise of others in the organization. Value is often affected by long-term considerations. Repetitive purchases may require a different perspective than one-time buys. What may constitute excellent value for one organization may not be good value for another, even if the prices and quantities are identical. For example, an organization facing an unexpected shortage may be willing to pay a substantial premium in price, or freight charges, to avoid an even more expensive stock-out or downtime. Another organization with greater lead time may work hard for a lower price or lower freight cost for an identical requirement.

A sound judgment as to what constitutes good value requires sensitivity to organizational objectives and priorities. The purchaser who unilaterally decides that a lower price is better than earlier delivery may not be making a decision in the best interest of his or her organization. Extensive consultations with the appropriate people in one's organization, be they in marketing, engineering, operations, finance or accounting, personnel, production, data processing, or maintenance, may be necessary to establish the appropriate trade-offs.

The notion as to what constitutes a "best buy" has been extensively covered in the traditional literature of the field. For example, Leenders, Fearon, and England[1] say:

> The decision on what to buy involves more than balancing various technical considerations. The most desirable technical quality or suitability for a given use, once determined, is not necessarily the desirable quality to buy. The distinction is between *technical quality,* which is strictly a matter of dimension, design, chemical, or physical properties and the like, and the more inclusive concept of *economic quality.* Economic quality assumes, of necessity, a certain minimum measure of suitability but considers cost and procurability as well.
>
> If the cost is so high as to be prohibitive, one must get along with an item somewhat less suitable. Or if, at whatever cost or however procurable, the only available suppliers of the technically perfect item lack adequate productive capacity or financial and other assurance of continued business existence, then, too, one must give way to something else. Obviously, too, frequent reappraisals are necessary although a workable balance between technical and economic quality has been established. If the price of copper increases from $0.90 a pound to $1.50 or more, its relationship to aluminum may change.
>
> The decision on what constitutes the best buy for any particular need is as much conditioned by procurement considerations as by technical quality. Best quality and best buy are one and the same. It should be clear that neither the engineer or user, on the one hand, nor the purchaser, on the other, is qualified to reach a sound decision on the best buy unless they work closely together. The ability and willingness of all parties concerned to view the trade-offs in perspective will significantly influence the final decisions reached.

Tools for determining best value include not only the full set of value analysis/engineering techniques, but also life cycle costing, purchasing research, "best practice" services, and so on.

Many reverse marketing examples encountered in this research stemmed from a purchaser's perception that the organization was not receiving good value using traditional procurement tools. There were quality, quantity, delivery, price, service, or other issues which created dissatisfaction with the status quo or with an expected future supply situation.

In many reverse marketing situations in the traditional context of no choice, the primary objective is probably supply assurance. Frequently, when other options do exist, the driving force behind reverse marketing is better economic value in terms of long-term ultimate cost to the organization. Ultimate cost recognizes that the price of the requirement is only one factor affecting the cost of the product or service produced. Ultimate cost, in this context is similar to life-cycle costs.

Since the primary procurement objective is to obtain sound value, it is not surprising that most reverse marketing examples stem from a value-driven motive.

Those who subscribe to the management philosophies of William Deming will recognize the extent to which purchasers may have to go to obtain good quality from vendors. Deming has a simple proposition that it must cost a supplier who produces no or very few rejects less to manufacture goods than a supplier who produces more rejects. Hence, the supplier who has the best quality should be able to offer the lowest price. It is interesting that the traditional procurement view is that it is reasonable to pay a premium price for better quality—a point undoubtedly not lost in the minds of industrial marketers! Many purchasers have found, however, that wanting better quality *and* price and getting both are two different things. For example, one electronics manufacturer found that only with an extensive period of education, testing, and supplier assistance, stretching over at least several years, was it able to move suppliers who showed potential to the stage where they could be consistently producing a quality product.

THE MALSTON EXAMPLE

The Malston Bakery situation described in Chapter 2 is an excellent example of a reverse marketing effort driven by value concerns, with price as the important individual factor. Since quality, quantity, delivery, and service from current suppliers were all excellent, the original concern focused solely on price. Bread flour was a major, repetitive requirement. Continually increasing flour costs were squeezing already thin margins. This caused the director of purchasing to start a major investigation. Even though he had purchased flour for many years, John Thomas had, heretofore, depended on market competition to set price levels. He therefore decided he was not sufficiently familiar with the milling process to understand the build-up of costs that occurred. His willingness to admit his own ignorance led to a series of visits to suppliers. What he found out strengthened his conviction that flour prices were too high. The visits also yielded another bonus, the idea that with fluctuating wheat and by-product prices, a cost-plus formula approach was reasonable to establish a fair miller's margin. Thus, John Thomas was now convinced that potential for value improvement existed and he had a means for determining a value fair to both purchaser and supplier. All he lacked was a willing supplier. It is interesting how often purchasers give existing suppliers a chance to come up with a better deal and how often existing suppliers pass up these opportunities. It is easy to see why, in the Malston case, where all suppliers were supporting an artificially high price level for flour, no one supplier would be anxious to upset the status quo. It was, therefore, up to the purchaser to provide enough pressure. In this case, the pressure had to come from a brand-new supplier, who was not part of the traditional supply network. Even so, it took a considerable amount of time for John Thomas to recognize the opportunity inherent in the Ross Mill. This probably arose because of his long-standing perception of the Ross Mill as only a soft flour supplier.

It is not unusual for purchasers to have a blind side with respect to certain vendors. Because a vendor has over a long period of time only supplied a certain product or line of items or services, the notion that this vendor might be capable of providing other requirements does not come easily. It is quite possible that, had John Thomas originally suggested a buy-out of the Ross Mill on the basis that bread flour making capacity be added, his initial proposal to the board of directors might have fared better than it did. Ironically, he got a second chance when Hellibell took over ownership of the mill. And, in the end, before the deal was finalized, John Thomas found himself insisting on a first right of refusal to buy the Ross Mill in case Hellibell wished to sell. By a circuitous route, Malston Bakery might eventually end up owning the Ross Mill and making bread flour itself, although the board of directors had originally vetoed the idea.

When price is a key consideration in value-driven reverse marketing, one significant advantage is the ease of determining success or failure, and the impact on the organization.

Even though improvement in other procurement objectives such as quality, quantity, delivery, and service can, of course, be quantified, it may require more effort and determination to trace through the real savings. In the flour case, it is easy to appreciate how large the savings to Malston turned out to be. John Thomas's strategy of using the Ross Mill to bring all suppliers into line on the price of bread flour not only resulted in annual savings close to $1 million, but also permitted his organization to compete effectively in a very tough market situation.

It is not uncommon to find that purchasing initiative to improve value is received coolly, or even negatively, by others in the organization. In Malston, the vice presidents of production and marketing immediately expressed doubts that satisfactory quality levels could be attained. This presented a dangerous potential trap for John Thomas. In his zeal to pursue his reverse marketing goal, he might have slipped and overstated the reality by making light of these objections. "Of course, quality will not be a problem" was a statement John Thomas could not, and did not, make. Instead, he had the wisdom of enlisting the assistance of both objectors in making sure that the quality would be acceptable. This helped the whole project, because, even though price was the original principal concern, satisfactory quality ultimately became the real hurdle the Ross Mill faced. All promises of future business were predicated on meeting the quality standards. And, with substantial assistance from Malston personnel, the Ross Mill managed to produce high-quality flour.

ASSISTANCE BY THE PURCHASER

It is usual in reverse marketing, particularly when the purchaser is larger than the supplier, for the vendor to require purchaser assistance. Success may not be possible without it, for several reasons. One reason a supplier may not already be providing what a purchaser really needs is that the supplier lacks the means. If the purchaser is perceptive enough to detect the shortcoming or potential roadblock to successful development, it is possible to address its resolution. In the Malston case, Paul Hellibell had several shortcomings. He and his organization had no experience with bread flour and his financial resources were limited. Normally, in a typical competitive bidding procurement stance, the Ross Mill would not even have been invited to quote for exactly these two reasons. And, without solutions to these obstacles, the Ross Mill could not be considered a viable source. The assistance in this case, a contract to guarantee cash flows, and technical expertise to guarantee quality, had to come from Malston.

In value-driven reverse marketing, the core, or the key must lie in the logic of the proposition. The purchaser must be able to perceive the economic benefits to the supplier and sell the proposal on that basis. In the Malston deal, John Thomas correctly assessed the new entrepreneur's desire to grow as an opportunity for both sides to get a good deal. Because Hellibell had not previously considered the possibility of getting into the bread flour business, he had no preconceived ideas as to price and market behavior. By being first to suggest a deal, John Thomas achieved a strategic position where *his* proposal was the basis for all subsequent discussion.

Another reverse marketing effort involving price was that of the Hudson Corporation. Sometimes a sole supplier, whose quality, service, and delivery may be excellent, does not come forth with price reductions or imposes unjustified price increases. In such cases, development of a second source at a lower price may push the initial supplier to reassess the price structure. The Hudson Corporation case, which follows, illustrates some of the issues that arise when a purchaser is concerned with achieving improved value from a sole source.

CASE: THE HUDSON CORPORATION

The Hudson Corporation specialized in the manufacture of hoisting equipment. The firm's principal product lines consisted of elevators and escalators, which it not only manufactured, but installed and maintained for customers as well. Its elevators and escalators could be found in most major cities in the world. After years of research, Hudson's engineers developed a new generation of computerized, low-energy hoisting equipment designed especially to eliminate almost all service work and to run almost noise-lessly. The new hoisting unit could be used in both manually oper-ated and automatic elevator systems. Close tolerances, uniformity of surface roughness, special "clean room" manufacturing tech-niques, and special alloys were all necessary requirements in the manufacture of the parts for the new hoisting units. The same basic design was used for all the company's elevators in fourteen different sizes of units to allow for demand variations in load, speed, and height. The drive mechanism of the new unit—which was sourced with an outside supplier—was produced offshore, im-ported into the country, and sold through a local subsidiary of the parent manufacturer. Even though the technology existed locally to produce the drive mechanisms, they were all imported and car-ried a high rate of duty. Hudson's sole supplier for the mecha-nism, Hamilton Inc., had provided excellent service for its drive mechanisms but balked at any suggestions by Hudson's pur-chasers for a price reduction on the units.

Mary Decarie, director of purchases for Hudson, became in-creasingly concerned about the growing volume of purchases of drive units and questioned why Hamilton could not initiate price breaks. The volume of hoisting units was increasing rapidly and new electronics technology should have allowed the cost per unit to drop. Decarie raised her concerns about price with executives of Hamilton on numerous occasions and received the same re-ply—they could make no price concessions. Decarie also tried to convince Hamilton to import the mechanism's components from its parent and assemble them locally, but to no avail. Although high tariffs existed on importing fully assembled units, there was no duty if parts were imported and assembled locally.

The attempt by Decarie to get Hamilton to move on price brought disdain from Hudson's chief engineer who explained that "anytime anything goes wrong with one of Hamilton's drive mechanisms on an elevator or escalator, or if we have a problem here, all we have to do is call them and they come running." Deca-rie replied: "Despite Hamilton's excellent service, they have not made any efforts to get their costs down. They continue to import complete units, to add their own margin, and to turn around and sell them to us." Hamilton's sales representatives had always dealt directly with Hudson's engineers and neither side saw any need to draw purchasing into any negotiations.

Decarie discussed her problem with the president of the National Hoisting Manufacturers' Association at a chance encounter, and the president suggested that Decarie talk to Jenkins Manufacturing, which had a local manufacturing facility, although, like Hamilton, all of its drive mechanisms were manufactured by its parent company offshore. When Decarie contacted the local Jenkins manufacturing facility and explained her desire to obtain a second source for hoisting drive mechanisms, ones that could be assembled locally to avoid duty, the response from Jenkins' top management was "We are very busy right now with our regular production. Why should we import the components and assemble the units for you here, when the principal benefactor appears to be your firm and not ours?"

During the following six months, Decarie worked simultaneously on her own engineering staff and on Jenkins's local management to try to convince them of the merit of her plan. To build her case she projected Hudson's demand for drive mechanisms during the next five years and emphasized that it was a growth market. Also she tried to convince Hudson's engineers that even with a second supplier, the increasing size of the market for hoisting equipment would actually cause purchases from Hamilton to increase, not decrease.

Hudson's chief engineer posed another problem: "What kind of cooperation exists between Jenkins's parent and local subsidiary? Just suppose Jenkins does get some business from us, what guarantees do we have that those units assembled locally will be of the same quality as those manufactured by the parent?" Replied Decarie: "Let's visit the Jenkins's parent and the local subsidiary and pose the same question to them." The Hudson engineers did this and were convinced that the same high quality could be produced locally. This removed the last serious engineering objections to Jenkins as a potential supplier.

The local managers of Jenkins were not sure they wanted the business, however. Decarie telephoned the sales manager at least once a month to remind him that Hudson was still interested in doing business with them.

About six months after her first visit to Jenkins, Decarie made her second visit. This time the plant manager was more optimistic. He said:

> We have had a chance to think this over and to discuss it with
> the various parties concerned in this company and the parent. It
> is obvious we will have to expand our facilities here sooner or

later. Taking your business now would hasten that expansion for us. Now, what kind of volume are you willing to give us and for how long?

Decarie said that she could give Jenkins a guaranteed 30 percent of Hudson's drive-unit business for the next five years, provided they produced a satisfactory trial order and that price was competitive with Hamilton. To the plant manager's question about what would happen after the first five years, Decarie replied: "What do you think is the future demand for hoisting equipment?"

After much negotiation by both parties, agreement was reached for a five-year contract with a minimum volume of 30 percent of Hudson's total purchases conditional on the satisfactory quality of an initial order of 40 units. The maximum original price for the machines was to be 5 percent below Hamilton's price. Jenkins was to import all the parts from its parent and assemble the units locally.

The initial order of 40 drive mechanisms was produced and proved completely satisfactory. Soon purchases from Jenkins met and exceeded the 30 percent minimum.

Shortly thereafter a salesman for Hamilton approached Decarie and told her, "A thorough cost improvement program has been instituted at our parent's plant and we have decided to pass on some of the savings to you by lowering our prices by eight percent."

Two weeks later the sales manager from Jenkins called to say that realized economies of scale were enabling a price reduction of 5 percent. Over the following months both Hamilton and Jenkins continued to make voluntary price reductions, each time ranging from 2 to 5 percent. A year after Jenkins was acquired as the second supplier, prices had dropped about 20 percent from Hamilton's original prices, and Hamilton had started to assemble the units locally, something they had always claimed they would never do.

Because of Hudson's efforts to decrease the import content of its products, Decarie was concerned that both Hamilton and Jenkins were still using imported parts in the units, although further price reductions were possible if each supplier found local suppliers for some of those parts. To confirm this belief, Decarie had her buyers analyze the drive mechanism units to suggest possible local suppliers for parts. The buyers estimated that by using local suppliers a substantial saving per unit could be realized.

When this point was raised with both Hamilton and Jenkins, each firm wanted to know how far Hudson intended to go with the local content push in an effort to reduce costs. Decarie's reply to both firms was:

> As far as we can. As long as it saves you money to make or buy locally, we would expect you to do so. We are not asking for one hundred percent local content, but where it produces savings, we both benefit. We are not asking you just to lower price, we expect you to make a satisfactory profit. We are sure, however, that you can have your profit and still lower the price if you follow what we suggest.

Both firms bought Decarie's idea and during the next year prices dropped another 10 percent, despite continuing increases in labor rates and raw material prices.

By now both suppliers were really competing for the business. Neither knew just what percentage of the total business each was getting. As it turned out, Hamilton did not lose out in total dollar volume as total demand increased sufficiently to cover all of the business supplied by Jenkins.

COMMENTS ON THE HUDSON CORPORATION CASE

The original need for reverse marketing stemmed from Hudson's desire for a second source of supply for a vital and major volume item. It is true that the original purchasing arrangement for elevator parts through engineering was not satisfactory from a procurement viewpoint. This consideration was definitely secondary, however, to the need for a second source of supply. Purchasing's careful handling of the situation actually resulted in solutions to both of these problems.

Convinced as she was of the need for a second supplier, Decarie deserves credit for her persistence in the face of all the resistance she encountered. There was a fast-growing demand for elevators and Decarie's efforts were made not in a buyer's but a seller's market.

The supplier's resistance actually came from two directions. The first objections came from the regular supplier who saw a favorable position threatened. In view of the later developments, one cannot help but think that this supplier had enjoyed not only a favored, but also a highly profitable position. The actual objections came in the form that might be expected in such a case:

What are you trying to do?

Have we not always given you good service?

Have we not always tried to please you?

Have we not gone out of our way to accommodate your special requests?

Decarie properly replied that service had been excellent, price performance had been poor, and volume had grown to the point where a second source made good procurement sense.

The new supplier's resistance came partially from the differences between the new units and its regular line. Its objections were again typical, however:

We are sure that this will save you some money, but what is really in it for us?

If you could wait a few years, it would make it much easier for us.

We are very busy right now; we have no room for anything like that.

Gradually, as the new supplier became more interested, new questions were asked—about guaranteeing the volume, regularity, and length of contract. These last items could be negotiated. The whole process was one of meeting each objection or problem with its own solution.

The same pattern was used to meet internal engineering resistance to the new reverse marketing. Engineering resistance was in a way more of a problem than the new supplier's resistance, because of engineering's fear of the purchasing department's intrusion into engineering affairs. Decarie's honest efforts to separate engineering and purchasing interests from company interests and to solve the basic problems, no matter who raised the objections, eventually won her engineering approval. Had she brushed aside legitimate engineering issues on the basis that all engineering objections were the results of sour grapes, her development probably would not have been successful. Valid engineering concern was expressed about the issues of quality and service. Another issue was whether the parent company would give the subsidiary all the technical assistance it needed. The nature of the new drive mechanisms was such that assembly and testing carried more pitfalls than seemed to be apparent. By examining the parent's willingness to extend that assistance, the purchaser also made clear to both the parent company and the subsidiary that she considered such assistance vital to the success of the project.

The issue of Hudson's basic company policy was involved in this supplier development. Hudson might have been able to pass on any of its costs to its customers. But Decarie considered it a duty of the purchasing department to reinforce the company's basic policy of giving the best value to its customers at the lowest possible prices. In view of the objections she encountered, her stance was even more admirable. It would have been easy to side-step the basic policy and moral issue to suit the expediency of the moment.

In this reverse marketing example Decarie used a stepping stone approach. All of the purchaser's first efforts were directed to the point where the new supplier became committed to try assembly of the new mechanisms. Decarie hoped that once the supplier had started, it would be possible to increase the total volume of business. This proved to be the case.

The resulting competition between the two sources of supply resulted in price reductions of about 20 percent. When prices stabilized, the purchaser started her second campaign, this time dealing with both suppliers, to reduce prices even further by substituting locally made items for high-cost imports. Both suppliers realized that refusal at this stage might lose them their competitive position. Even here, the basic logic of the purchaser's position was clear:

> We are not asking you to lower prices for our sake alone.
>
> We are positive you can make the same machine for us just as well, but less expensively, if you don't import all the parts.
>
> We have already analyzed this possible area ourselves and we can suggest right now some of the more obvious examples.
>
> You will save us money, but you will still be able to make a satisfactory profit.

Both suppliers realized that the purchaser was again trying to get her foot inside the door for the purpose of leverage later on. The original supplier immediately asked the critical question "How far are you going to push us on this one?" With the proper reply, "As long as it will do both of us some good." The purchaser put the responsibility for cost reduction back with the supplier. The resulting price reductions in the years thereafter showed that the reverse marketing had been completely successful.

ADDITIONAL EXAMPLES

Another example paralleling Hudson Corporation's experience was that of a firm whose sole supplier of wirebound boxes imposed price increases of 6 percent every four months for a year and a half, followed by a 13 percent increase. As the purchaser's final product was sold at a fixed price for one year, it was impossible to pass the supplier's frequent increases along to the final customer. After an initial search, an offshore supplier was located that had an FOB purchaser's plant price at a 15 percent saving. When the purchaser cut the original supplier's volume by 50 percent, that supplier canceled its most recent 13 percent increase. The increased competition caused by the introduction of the second supplier resulted in a great increase in quality as well.

A different approach in the quest for better value was pursued by a municipality that purchased large quantities of lapel pins, police, fire, and ambulance identification badges, and presentation items such as award medals. The items were all metal and handpainted with a resulting high labor content due to the number of colors of enamels used on each item. The purchaser questioned the use of metal for the items and while investigating possible alternatives encountered an attractive plastic that could be injected with different colors. The patented supplier was able to replicate the most intricate lapel pin and badge at one-third the cost of metal. However, the manufacturer was reluctant to produce the items because of the low volume. It was only after the municipality's purchasers used their broad contacts with other potential buyers to develop a sufficient demand for the new items that the supplier would consent to commence full-scale production.

A unique quest for better value was demonstrated by a gas utility company that was dissatisfied with its sole source for gas compressors and spare parts for its liquid natural gas plants. Due to the special nature of gas plant parts and components, the purchaser sensed a monopolistic attitude by the manufacturer/supplier. The reverse marketing initiative consisted of contacting several of the manufacturer/supplier's parts and components suppliers to convince them to supply unique parts to the sole-source supplier's competition. Support was enlisted from other gas utilities resulting in a worthwhile market.

These examples of the purchaser's quest for better value, although diverse in approach, all have a common theme—the route traveled is seldom smooth and the current supplier does not volunteer better value options. Reverse marketing was necessary to bring pressure on the existing supplier and to prove that lower prices were possible.

BRIEF SUMMARY

1. Value is the key objective of reverse marketing.

2. Obtaining a better price is often an objective.

3. Purchasers normally initiate price negotiations with current suppliers, giving them a first chance.

4. Normally, current suppliers rebuff such initiatives.

5. The purchaser may have to find an "outside" vendor who is not preconditioned to existing pricing practices and price levels.

6. The purchaser's proposal becomes the basis for negotiation: therefore, the purchaser must prove that the proposed price is viable.

7. Reverse marketing may be used to create a competitive climate.

8. Supplier assistance may be necessary (especially with small suppliers).

9. Internal resistance is likely.

10. A long-term view is essential.

11. The purchaser must be persistent.

CHAPTER 4

Technology and Reverse Marketing

TECHNOLOGY and reverse marketing are closely linked. The purchaser's organization may be planning to introduce a new technology into its management system, process, products, or services offered. A requirement for a supplier who can meet this technological challenge well is thus generated. On the other hand, suppliers may be developing new materials, products, processes, or services, and the purchaser may be anxious to reap the benefits. Reverse marketing may be necessary to assure the purchaser early or timely access to such technology. In certain situations, securing suppliers who will be on the leading edge of new technology may be one of the key success factors of the organization. Technology is so pervasive that it is useful to examine reverse marketing involving technology issues.

The case that follows illustrates the use of reverse marketing when a firm is not satisfied with the current level of technology available in its industry and tries to do something about it.

CASE: MEGA TECHNOLOGIES INC.

Mega Technologies produced special parts for packaging machines. Automated packaging equipment is used by consumer goods companies producing beer, liquor, shampoo, mouthwash, and the like, and is available from a number of packaging equipment manufacturers throughout the world. The parts produced by Mega positioned containers to be filled or helped orient containers for label application. Mega also manufactured some very special specialized packaging equipment and performed some packaging equipment overhaul work.

Paul Hill, the firm's president, pondered how he could obtain a competitive edge. He felt that his firm's current products were superior to those produced by the competition, whose products were plagued by inconsistency of quality and design defects. However, even the latest generation of machines available to produce packaging machine components did not have the flexibility to produce all the different required variations needed and to handle the complexities presented by firms with unique packaging problems. Mr. Hill, a graduate of a well-known engineering school with a world-wide reputation in computers, pondered the idea of applying computer technology to the traditional machinery used in his industry, whose technology had seen little change for the past decade.

The Mega line of component parts was incomplete—the firm did not manufacture cams and feedscrews, which were a vital component in packaging equipment. Also, Paul Hill had visions of becoming the leader in his highly competitive field. He felt that the application of computer technology had the potential to leap-frog Mega ahead of its competitors. If this objective could be realized, it would complete Mega's product line, give the firm more product line flexibility and in-house control, and place Mega ahead of its competition.

The major innovation in machines that produced cams and feedscrews had occurred with the introduction of numerically controlled (NC) equipment, which used tapes up to 1000 feet long for control. Any changes in the machine's operations would require a new tape because the machine had no capability to make changes internally. The next generation, called computer controlled, could be instructed with codes or commands. The computer-controlled generation became user friendly, used a 200 foot tape instead of a 1000 foot tape, but still did not have the capability to do sophisticated work. Whereas the numerically controlled machines took one month to program, and the computer-controlled machines took one week, the new generation of computer-controlled machines envisioned by Paul Hill would initially take one day to program, with that time being cut to 20 minutes within a year of perfecting the machine. The cost savings and flexibility associated with the reduced programming time were of particular interest to Paul Hill. He envisioned the necessity for two machines, one to manufacture cams and the other feedscrews. Hill estimated that the cost to develop these machines would be as follows:

Capital cost of the machines	$ 800,000
Support equipment	150,000
Changes to current facilities	80,000
Software costs	200,000
	$1,230,000

This figure did not include any cost for the time of Paul Hill and other Mega employees who would work on the project.

Paul Hill then approached five major North American equipment manufacturers. Several of these firms initially showed enthusiasm for the project but soon lost interest when they realized its complexity and the commitment required. Six months later, when Paul Hill mentioned his frustration about this to the salesperson of a speciality equipment manufacturing firm, he received an interesting lead. The salesperson suggested the name of a German equipment manufacturer that had done some work using the technology described by Mr. Hill, although in vastly different types of machines. Paul Hill immediately telephoned the German firm, Rhone AG, and explained his ideas about applying computer technology to traditional equipment. After several months of exchanging ideas, it became apparent to Mr. Hill that Rhone AG understood the problems Mega Technologies was facing. Upon his suggestion, Helmut Schmidt, a Rhone AG technical expert, visited the Mega plant. It soon became apparent that although Schmidt understood computer applications for machinery, he had no background in feedscrew technology and Hill had to give him an orientation to the field.

It was at this point that agreement in principle with Rhone AG was reached to go ahead with the project. However, there were still several major hurdles to overcome, the biggest of which was financial. A delay ensued when the bank that had initially agreed to finance the project backed out, leaving Paul Hill to seek alternate financing.

Rhone AG was a large manufacturer of specialized machinery with a reputation for being aggressive in developing new types of equipment. The firm possessed unique technology which was un-available in North America. It had developed on-board machine computers based on mathematical equations which greatly re-duced the amount of manual input required in machine setup and operation. The firm had as its customers large, well-known firms such as Volkswagen and Rolls Royce, but was reluctant to use these large firms as a proving ground for new ideas. The initiative by Mega Technologies presented an opportunity for Rhone to form a partnership to experiment with the new technology before attempting to sell it to its major customers. Moreover, Rhone AG had been seeking a way to gain a presence in the North American market and cooperation with Mega would be a first step in this direction. Also Rhone AG did not have the sophisticated level of computer technology possessed by Mega and viewed a liaison with Mega as a chance to obtain this technology. In addition, the agree-ment with Mega called for the purchase of two machines by Mega, one for cams and one for feedscrews.

As the project progressed beyond the preliminary stages, Rhone AG had problems in integrating the old technology feedscrew ma-chine with computer technology. Now it was Hill's turn to try to understand Rhone's problems and propose solutions. Overcoming these difficulties took time.

Since a computer was at the heart of the new machine, Paul Hill knew it was crucial that a match be made with the right com-puter firm at an early stage in the project. Also, since he realized the importance of an ongoing liaison with the computer manufac-turer after the machine was constructed, he preferred the idea of involving a large, well-known firm with a European presence. As he sought advice from firms that used computer control equip-ment, the company most frequently mentioned was the High-Tech Computer Company (High-Tech), which had an excellent record in working with computers in machines of this type.

When they learned that Paul Hill wanted High-Tech to provide the computer input, Rhone AG contacted the German High-Tech subsidiary in Hamburg, although Rhone had done a lot of in-house computer work themselves and had an ongoing relationship with a Japanese manufacturer for computer hardware. High-Tech, Hamburg, saw the joint venture with Rhone and Mega as a potential learning experience coupled with an opportunity to se-cure a new large customer in Rhone AG.

The development of the new machine was now a three-way affair—Rhone AG and High-Tech were working jointly with Mega acting as a catalyst.

After three years of development and testing and many transatlantic conversations and visits, the first new machine was delivered to Mega. Just prior to its delivery, Mr. Hill discovered while on a fact-finding mission to Japan, that the Japanese had successfully integrated the same two technologies which had resulted in a machine quite similar to the new Rhone–High-Tech–Mega one.

Subsequent Events

This reverse marketing project provided Hill with a new machine that enabled Mega to produce a better product and thus attract new customers. The project also gained Mega industry recognition as being on the leading edge of packaging technology which helped other segments of its business. Furthermore, there were benefits from the project that Hill had not anticipated. He had not envisioned that the new generation of machines would have the capability to produce specialty screws; the machine had more flexibility than originally envisioned. The reverse marketing exercise also forced Mega to put together a long-range marketing plan and strategy—something the firm had not previously done.

Despite these benefits, Paul Hill wondered in retrospect just how much time and effort Mega had put into the project and decided to try to put an estimate on it. He remembered that he had spent a great deal of time on the project from the conception of the idea in year 1 through ordering the equipment from Rhone AG in year 2 until the first machine was delivered late in year 3 (6 months late). After delivery of this machine, 50 percent of his time was involved with the machine, while another Mega employee was involved 100 percent on the project. In addition, a salesperson sold the product produced by the new machine and two people were hired to run the machine. At this point the firm was particularly vulnerable if they lost an employee. A year or so later Hill still spent a significant amount of time selling the product and assisting in the resolution of tricky technological problems.

Rhone AG introduced similar machines for sale to the packaging industry, although Mega had secured an agreement that Rhone AG would not sell the exact Mega machine to another customer. The technology was also now available from Japanese and other equipment manufacturers. As the new machine was being developed, Paul Hill had not pushed to have it patented as he felt that once something was patented it became public knowledge. Mega's competitors were reluctant to purchase the new machines from Rhone AG because of their high initial cost and the modifications that would have to be made to suit each individual buyer.

Rhone AG was able to utilize features developed for the new Mega machine in other machines that it produced. For example, the "reading head" developed for the Mega machine, which contained a computer that stored information, was being built into new-generation Rhone machines. Also, in developing the Mega machine, because of the many read-outs generated by the computer, the need for a CRT (cathode ray tube) was examined. As a result of the "experimenting" with the Mega machine, the second-generation Rhone machines had a CRT integrated into them. The reverse marketing experience with Mega generated additional sales

FIGURE 4–1.
Mega Technologies: Chronological Steps
in the Reverse Marketing Project

Time Period	Activity
1. Beginning year 1	Conceptualization
2. First seven months of year 1	Concept and technology discussions with vendors Preliminary sourcing attempts rebuffed
3. Last five months of year 1	New sourcing internationally— ultimately successful. Machines ordered.
4. Beginning of year 3	First machine delivered 6 months late Debugging period started for first machine
5. Beginning of year 4	Second machine delivered 12 months late Debugging period started for second machine
6. Late year 4 and beginning of year 5	Machine modifications on both machines
7. By end of year 7	Twelve changes in software, 6 - 8 significant changes in the machines

by Rhone AG to both Rolls Royce and Volkswagen of machines utilizing the new technology.

A chronological summary of the main steps of this reverse marketing is shown in Figure 4–1.

REVERSE MARKETING INSIGHTS FROM MEGA TECHNOLOGIES

The Mega example highlights aspects of reverse marketing which surface when new technology is involved. Reverse marketing involving new technology is obviously not restricted to large firms with large research and development departments and many resources at their disposal. Mega was a small firm under an owner-manager with very limited financial resources.

While the initial reason for embarking on this project was to fill a gap in Mega's product line—cams and feedscrews—there existed a deeper motivation beyond simply a financial one. Paul Hill had a desire that his firm be known in the industry as a leader in new technology. He also felt that success in this project would propel the growth of his firm.

Paul Hill acted as a catalyst in this project. He was successful in bringing together two much larger firms in different industries, computers and machinery manufacturing, to work toward a common goal. He also was a technologically sophisticated purchaser. Because Mega was a small firm, the president, Paul Hill, embodied the marketing, engineering, purchasing, and upper management functions in one person, himself. In a larger firm these functions would most likely be located in separate departments, making decision making slower and increasing the need for coordination.

One would also expect that in larger firms the initiative for the new technology would originate within a marketing, engineering, research and development, or production group. At what time the purchasing function would get involved would depend on the particular policies and strengths and weaknesses of the organization. One might consider it a lucky chance that, thanks to Paul Hill's perseverance, he did get a lead on the German firm. Until a potential supplier had been found, the project was effectively stalled at the concept stage.

Given the range of Paul Hill's duties, it was not possible for him to engage in a fully systematic world-wide supplier search. He did test the North American market, but did not have the time to search beyond. It is possible that, had he turned to Japanese suppliers, the need for his extensive personal involvement might not have been so great. As it was, the Japanese on their own developed basically the same technology.

Obviously, thanks to his intimate involvement, Paul Hill had a grasp of the technology, its potential and problems, that would be very difficult to duplicate for someone who simply purchased the new machines once they became available in the marketplace. Even so, extensive modifications and testing took place after the machines had been delivered, further delaying the time of real payoff to Mega.

Because he was vitally involved in all facets of the reverse marketing project, Hill was able to inject enthusiasm and keep morale high among all those involved. He was the product champion in this case. However, this enthusiasm and dedication did not come without cost. Hill found that he spent a great deal of his time and energy on the project and he felt that it had aged him considerably.

GENERAL OBSERVATIONS ABOUT THE PROJECT

The Mega project was a high-risk one. It is not evident that Paul Hill seriously assessed the various risks, technological and commercial, that this reverse marketing effect entailed. The consequences of failure could have been severe for Mega, both financially and psychologically. And it may be questioned whether the benefits to Mega were worth the effort. The appearance of Japanese equipment on the market at about the same time the first Mega machine was delivered further underscores this point. One can only speculate as to what other projects Paul Hill might have undertaken instead of this one. Neither is it clear what results he might have achieved with such alternate efforts. The payoff to Mega was relatively modest. It received two pieces of equipment, which allowed it to enter into the cam and feedscrew markets. Paul Hill did not even receive royalties or patent fees for any of his ideas which he freely shared with Rhone and High-Tech. It would be interesting to speculate how a much larger purchasing firm would have handled this effort and all of its commercial aspects.

The Mega case suggests a number of implications for reverse marketing, should technology be a key aspect. Obviously, the need to define well the new technology's capabilities is front and center. Also, however, there is a need to assess the new technology's impact on the organization as a whole. In the Mega case, corporate growth, corporate reputation, and access to new markets were all part of the whole picture. This integration of a technological and organizational perspective was relatively easy for Mega, since Paul Hill was the president of the firm. His purchasing skills did not match his technical prowess. He did not comb the North American market for alternatives, and accepted the first suggestion he received for a foreign source. A more extensive search might have convinced him that there was no need to involve himself and his firm so deeply, since the equipment would appear on the market in due course. What is particularly striking is the length of time for the whole effort, and the extensive need for communication throughout the development, compared to a more standard, value-driven reverse marketing project. The total project stretched over about seven years, and, on the part of Mega alone, required a number of person years to complete.

In this example, the need to go beyond national and traditional trading area boundaries was apparent. This may suggest that, even though local options might exist, there could be wisdom in assessing the technology world-wide before making a commitment. Much as a local source might have been preferred for ease of communication, the technological strength of the vendor dictated going offshore.

Not unique to new technology is the phenomenon of local supplier reluctance. If one sees the benefits to Rhone of Mega's effort, it is easy to see the opportunity local vendors passed up when Paul Hill gave them first shot at the idea. Is it possible that they saw Mega as a risky, small customer, and did not appreciate the unique personal skills and vision of Paul Hill? The long-term result was that their foreign competition increased through greater technological strength. In the long run, the five North American firms which refused Paul Hill's original offer ended up being the real long-term losers.

It can be argued that the two suppliers that Paul Hill developed—Rhone AG and High-Tech—gained more by the experience than did Mega Technologies. Rhone AG increased its credibility in the computer-aided machine field which resulted in sales to both Rolls Royce and Volkswagen of machines utilizing the new technology. Furthermore, the firm was able to gain a foothold in the North American market, something it had been attempting to do for some time. High-Tech also gained by the project, increasing its access to the European market and ensuring a solid future for its computers in succeeding generations of Rhone-produced machines. The benefits to these two suppliers clearly went well beyond the Mega order.

This example also showed the need for purchaser and supplier to stay in constant communication. Paul Hill assigned himself the task of project leader, visionary, and technological expert. It was he who envisioned the final result better than anyone else involved. Yet despite the continuity of his role throughout the project, the equipment was delivered late and required major modifications in both hardware and software in the years following installation. It is ironic that Mega's competitors did not fully grasp the potential benefits of the new equipment, even when it was offered them on a silver platter, so to speak. They were not sufficiently technologically sophisticated to appreciate the potential of the new equipment, or to be able to use it well. Thus, the main benefit to Mega as the purchaser and developer of the new technology was, perhaps, the knowledge gained during the reverse marketing process. It was the combination of this knowledge and the equipment purchased that helped propel Mega to industry leadership. It may well be that the process of overcoming the technological challenges that arise in reverse marketing produces the technological edge the purchaser seeks to acquire.

The Mega Technologies case involved a small purchaser with two large suppliers. In the following example of Panelectronics Inc., a large purchaser is involved with both a small and large supplier in the development of a new technology.

CASE: PANELECTRONICS INC.

Founded in 1908 in Chicago, Panelectronics Inc., had grown to become one of North America's largest and best-known telecommunications equipment manufacturers. Its product line included a full range of state-of-the-art telecommunications equipment which was constantly being augmented with new product offerings.

Panelectronics had started a company-wide effort to increase the U.S. content of its products. Obviously, the supply function was heavily involved in the program. Carol French, vice president of materials, was a firm believer in U.S. industry's potential to produce almost anything Panelectronics imported. She would not shift from imports to U.S. sources, however, unless it was to the advantage of Panelectronics. She found that she could get far better results in many cases if she sought out U.S. suppliers rather than waiting for them to come to her. The following example involving the purchase of a special part with electromagnetic properties illustrates the need for perseverance at the start, for financial and technological assistance, and for a stepping-stone approach.

Watson Company: Inability to Overcome Technical Problems

Part #503, with special electromagnetic properties was one of the imported items for which Ms. French had been unable to find a U.S. supplier. Yearly purchases from an offshore supplier amounted to $1.2 million, with each part costing $9. Part #503 was made of acoloy, a special alloy with such strong magnetic retention that over a period of 20 years, it lost less than 1 percent of its original magnetism.

The manufacture of part #503 was a difficult and highly technical operation. The offshore supplier made part #503 by feeding a preheated strip of white-hot acoloy into a press with a three-cavity die. Preheating of the acoloy strip required the use of large induction coils which traveled with the strip right up to the point of impact. The temperature of the strip was about 1500°C. Panelectronics engineers considered making part #503 in their own shop but they estimated that the relatively low volume would not warrant the high development and investment costs required.

Ms. French searched for a possible U.S. supplier, and subsequently found Watson Company, a small firm which specialized in unusual alloys required in small quantities. Ms. French went to see the sales manager of Watson Company at the plant in Detroit. The sales manager was interested in part #503 and called in the head of the engineering department. Ms. French explained to him that Panelectronics' engineers had investigated the possibility of manufacturing part #503 in Panelectronics' own plant, but that they had decided against it. Should Watson Company, because of its familiarity with small-lot production of special alloys, be in a better position to make part #503, Panelectronics would be happy to give them the business. The sales manager and the head of engineering thanked Ms. French for coming to them and said that they would discuss the problem with others in their company. Several weeks later the sales manager telephoned Ms. French and told her that Watson Company would be interested in giving part #503 a try. Ms. French made several appointments for Watson Company engineers to come and discuss the manufacturing process with the Panelectronics engineers who had worked on the first investigation.

At a subsequent meeting in her office, Ms. French and the sales manager of Watson came to a formal agreement. Panelectronics would provide what technical help they could, and would test all samples for Watson. It would pay $7.25 for each sample and agreed to buy part #503 from Watson should they be able to develop a satisfactory product at a satisfactory price.

In a letter to the Watson Company sales manager Ms. French confirmed these terms. A further paragraph in the letter stated:

> Pleased as I am with your company's decision to go ahead with development of part #503, I still wish to caution you that our commitment to buy part #503 depends entirely on your ability to produce a satisfactory product. I view your decision to undertake this project as a sharing of the risks involved. Your risk is that your development will not be successful, with the result that much of your time and money will be wasted. Our risk is that if you are unable to produce a satisfactory product, we will have needlessly spent large amounts of our time and money in the testing of our samples and unsuccessful reverse marketing. I am apprehensive because our own engineers decided they could not tackle the project. I do, however, sincerely hope your efforts will be successful.

Watson produced its first samples several months later. Panelectronics sent about $6000 of testing equipment to Watson so that their engineers could test for some of the magnetic properties in their own plant. Panelectronics' engineers set up the testing equipment and taught Watson's engineers how to use it. Other tests were carried out by including samples in actual product production. Failure of these samples resulted in a loss of $54 for each sample to Panelectronics because of the labor costs involved in part #503 assembly and replacement and the parts cost of the assembly itself. The assembly could not be disassembled after it had been put together and a faulty part #503 would cause the complete loss of the whole assembly.

Watson engineers had decided that the current method of manufacture required too large an investment in equipment to be suited for the small quantity Panelectronics needed. They therefore tried casting, using the shell-molding process. This proved to be another difficult technical feat. Flow point control of acoloy was extremely critical. A few degrees too high or too low would seriously affect the magnetic properties of the final product. For a year and a half Watson continued trying to perfect this method of producing part #503. During that time, Panelectronics engineers repeatedly visited the Watson plant and tried to be of service in testing samples and suggesting changes. Hundreds of samples were tested and found deficient. Watson was unable to produce part #503 to Panelectronics' specifications.

After about two years, the president of Watson decided to call a halt to further part #503 development work. He sent a letter to Ms. French asking for reimbursement of the $90,000 development cost which Watson had incurred in working on the project. Ms. French wrote back saying it was her understanding that Watson would pay for its own development work and that Panelectronics had no intention of paying anything.

Ms. French heard nothing for several weeks. Then one day she received a telephone call from the president of Panelectronics who said: "Ms. French, I have two gentlemen in my office from Watson who claim we owe them $90,000. They say you refuse to pay them. Will you please come to my office?"

Ms. French took out the Watson vendor file and went to the president's office. There she found the president and sales manager of Watson. Panelectronics' president said: "Now that Ms. French is here, would you mind explaining again why you came to see me?"

The president of Watson said:

> Ms. French came to our company about two years ago to see if she could interest Watson in producing part #503. We agreed to do the development work for Panelectronics and have since incurred expenses totalling $90,000 on this project. Although we were unsuccessful in producing a product that met with your

specifications, we do think you should reimburse us for the expenses we incurred.

Panelectronics' president said: "How about it, Ms. French?"

Ms. French replied:

> It is true that I went to Watson to ask them to produce part #503. I did not commit Panelectronics to any payment for development work aside from the $7.25 payment per sample. Although Watson Company claims to have spent $90,000 of this project, I am sure it has cost Panelectronics just as much when you consider the cost of our engineers' time, the test equipment, and the hundreds of faulty part #503 assemblies we had to scrap at a cost of $54 each to us. My understanding was that Watson and Panelectronics would share the risk of development on this basis. I confirmed this view in a letter to the sales manager of Watson Company two years ago.

Ms. French then read the letter including the paragraph referred to above.

Before anyone else could say anything, after Ms. French had read this letter, the president of Watson stood up and said: "I am very sorry we came to bother you. Thank you for your time and explanation." Both Watson representatives left immediately.

Vencor Inc.: Development of a New Product

With the failure of the reverse marketing project with Watson, Carol French was still not satisfied that she had fully examined all the alternatives, and continued her efforts.

About six months after the last Watson visit, Ms. French discussed part #503 with one of her purchasing managers. Ms. French said that she thought the chances of getting acoloy manufactured in the United States seemed unlikely and wondered if perhaps another approach should be tried. "Perhaps we should be looking for another alloy with the same magnetic properties but not as temperamental in manufacture," she suggested. This was one approach the engineers had discounted right from the start. They knew that acoloy had been especially developed for this application after many years of research. They also knew that no other alloy commercially available came even close to having acoloy's properties.

FIGURE 4–2.
Panelectronics Incorporated Chronological Steps
in the Reverse Marketing Project

Time Period	Activity
Early in year 1	Panelectronics' company-wide effort to increase U.S. content of its products. This was followed shortly by Ms. French's discovery of the Watson Company as a potential supplier for part #503
June 17, year 1	Agreement in principle reached with Watson Company
June 18, year 1	Letter to Watson Company formalizing the agreement
September, year 1	First samples of part #503 produced by Watson Company
September, year 1 - February, year 3	Hundreds of samples of part #503 were tested and found deficient
February, year 3	Watson Company stopped part #503 development work. Letter sent requesting $90,000 in development costs
March 10, year 3	Meeting with Ms. French, Panelectronics' president, and the president and sales manager of Watson Company
September, year 3	Ms. French discussed the part #503 problem with one of her buyers
September, year 3	Sales representative of Vencor contacted
October, year 3	Formal agreement reached with Vencor, similar to that with Watson Company
October, year 3 - September, year 4	Progress made on part #503 with successive batches of alloy
October, year 5	Breakthrough with Venco 555X
January, year 6	First shipment of part #503 sent to Panelectronics

Ms. French, nevertheless, asked her purchasing manager to discuss the problem with the sales representative of Vencor Inc., one of the largest U.S. nonferrous metal producers. Vencor Inc. research had led to the well-known Venco alloys which in the 500 series had been specifically developed for their magnetic properties. The highest alloy in the Venco 500 series was Venco 540; the others were numbers 510, 520, and 530. Ms. French discussed the qualities of the Venco 500 alloys with Panelectronics engineers.

The engineers explained that the Venco equivalent to acoloy should be about Venco 595, a long way from their closest approximation, Venco 540. Panelectronics' purchasing manager discussed the problem with the Vencor sales representatives who promised to talk to the people in the plant about it. Several months later the purchasing manager informed Ms. French that Vencor's vice president of sales wished to discuss part #503. A meeting was held and Ms. French again promised Panelectronics help in the form of testing and engineering time. Vencor's laboratories produced successive batches of alloy which were cast and then machined. After about a year it became obvious that progress was being made. The faults of each previous batch were eliminated with each following batch, and Panelectronics' engineers working on the project became optimistic.

Almost two years after the first approach to Vencor, the head of research at Vencor told Panelectronics' engineers:

> As far as we are concerned we have found the equivalent to acoloy in our Vencor alloy series. Our Venco 555x has far fewer problems in manufacture and still has all of the electrical and magnetic properties you are interested in.

Several months of thorough testing by Panelectronics' engineers confirmed that Venco 555x was a suitable substitute for acoloy. Shortly thereafter Vencor sent its first shipment of part #503 to Panelectronics at a price of $2.52 each, a saving of $6.48 per part.

Figure 4–2 outlines the chronological steps taken by Panelectronics in its reverse marketing project.

OBSERVATIONS ON PANELECTRONICS' REVERSE MARKETING EFFORTS

This example shows how a supplier with a different technology can effect large dollar savings. The price of part #503 to Panelectronics was reduced from $9.00 to $2.52 resulting in an annual saving of about $840,000.

In Ms. French's first attempt at reverse marketing for part #503, it was unfortunate that technological problems involved in casting acoloy proved to be too great for the Watson Company. Perhaps they should never have started on this project. Surely one of the danger signals right from the start was Panelectronics' decision not to attempt part #503 manufacture itself. For this reason, Ms. French might be questioned in her decision to involve a small supplier. On the other hand, Ms. French was absolutely honest about the problems she envisaged in the manufacture of part #503. Her statement of this in writing to the supplier made this warning doubly clear. The frustration of the supplier at not being able to develop satisfactory samples can be appreciated. Watson's attempt to recoup development costs may be seen as an extension of this frustration. Both purchaser and supplier started their agreement in good faith. Regrettably, the technical development problems involved in part #503 were too great for the limited resources of the small supplier.

On the other hand, the larger supplier turned out to have the research strength in alloys and development ability that the small supplier and Panelectronics lacked. It was able to carry on the development required and after eight months progress was evident. Vencor had all the advantages of a larger supplier and Panelectronics was able to benefit from this. The ultimate direct saving on an original order of $1,200,000 per year was about $840,000 per year, a large dollar amount, and an excellent reason for purchaser persistance in this originally unsuccessful effort. The uncertain nature of the research results prevented any purchaser price commitment until the final approval had been received from Panelectronics' testing engineers.

The part #503 example shows that for certain types of research and development work a larger supplier may be the better source. This was also true in the Mega Technologies example. Watson, a relatively small supplier, was willing to undertake the project but may not have been the best choice under the circumstances; perhaps Ms. French should not have chosen the firm. The ability of Watson to sustain a loss in case of failure may have been in question. Thus, although Ms. French was obviously in the clear legally, her initial choice may not have been the best. This is, of course, easily said with perfect hindsight. Nevertheless, in reverse marketing it should be the responsibility of the purchaser to foresee the range of consequences that might befall a supplier. It is not sufficient to protect the risk of exposure only of the purchaser in such situations.

The issue of who pays for the costs incurred in reverse marketing was clearly demonstrated by Watson Company's initial refusal to absorb its agreed-upon share. Ms. French's wise move of having the oral agreement supported by a letter paid off when disagreement of costs later arose. Especially in reverse marketing involving new technology, the issue of who is responsible for what costs and what risks is one that requires resolution at the start.

In this sequence of reverse marketing, first with the Watson Company and then with Vencor, the initiative came from the purchaser. Even though Panelectronics had strong engineering and R&D departments, it was the relatively simple suggestion from Ms. French that a different alloy might represent a better direction in which to search that opened up new avenues. The technological strengths of Ms. French were certainly limited in comparison to those who were experts in the field. Her willingness to think about the situation in a common-sense, managerial perspective helped the project along at a time when it appeared to be stalled. The opportunity for an inquisitive and persistent purchaser to make contributions in reverse marketing situations involving high or special technology should, therefore, not be minimized.

It is equally obvious that the remainder of this development effort required the special technical skills of Vencor and Panelectronics experts to achieve the desired results.

OTHER TECHNOLOGY-DRIVEN
REVERSE MARKETING EXAMPLES

Avco-Everett Inc., a large U.S. firm engaged in R&D and one-of-a-kind high-tech items utilizes a concept called a "Scientific Symposium" as a preliminary step in its reverse marketing program. The Scientific Symposium consists of a series of meetings between Avco's scientific personnel and purchasing to address issues involved in dealing with potential supplier firms in the high-tech field. It is felt that the symposium might elicit common characteristics of past purchasers, past supplier track records, and other input relating to new developments and new firms in the field—all of which might be used to facilitate identification of firms with which to engage in reverse marketing.

Texas Instruments Inc. uses its "design-to-cost" concept effectively with new high-tech products. The firm starts with a defined need in a product and the final price of the product that will satisfy that need including the assumption of a learning curve–based cost performance by the vendor. Suppliers are then solicited to help develop the product within the final product-price constraints in an informal partnership with Texas Instruments.

Also, when the Japanese inventor of vacuum fluorescent displays—used by Texas Instruments on microwave ovens—didn't have the capability to develop the device for other uses (such as toys and games), Texas Instruments participated in the development of additional sources of supply for the device. Because of this, the original display faces on Texas Instruments calculators, called maxi-tubes, were replaced by the vacuum fluorescent tube.

In another example, a paint company spent $2.5 million per year on a specialty chemical. Significant supply complications arose with the offshore supplier of this chemical. Upon investigation it was found that local chemical and oil companies such as Union Carbide, Shell, and Gulf had new-technology plants that produced feedstocks which might allow for production of the chemical in question. The task at hand was to identify exactly what by-products were coming out of the new refineries and chemical plants and to determine whether the necessary feedstocks were present to allow for production of the required chemical. Simply highlighting new end uses for some of their by-products encouraged these firms to further investigate areas of interest for the paint company. The end result was that the paint company secured a local source of supply and the chemical and oil companies secured new markets for their by-products.

REVERSE MARKETING AND NEW TECHNOLOGY

New technology, unlike many other opportunities, offers the potential of major leaps forward in competitive position, or substantial price improvements. These benefits are likely to have significant impact on the organization's ability to survive and prosper. Therefore, reverse marketing involving new technology is likely to require a full corporate, rather than just a purchasing effort.

On the other hand, reverse marketing involving new technology may take a long time, be complex, and require a world-wide supplier search, strong cross-functional efforts within the purchasing organization, and special expertise.

Both vendor and purchaser need to worry about the total costs of failure and who will be responsible for which costs should such failure occur. One of the classic examples involving new technology is that of Rolls Royce whose difficulties in developing a new engine for Lockheed's new aircraft placed both companies in jeopardy. The significance of new technology to organizational welfare may be such that a task force approach is the only reasonable way to proceed. A high profile project leader and continuity of personnel both in the purchasing and supplying organizations will also be required.

In a research effort independent of this reverse marketing research, Roger A. More studied developer/adopter relationships from an industrial marketing perspective.[1] Thus, in his language, the developer is the supplier who is trying to introduce a new industrial product. Excerpts from his conclusions show that in technology-based industrial product organizations there is frequently a need to manage a complex relationship with the purchasing organization. In other words, if the purchaser does not take the initiative in this relationship, the supplier may pursue a cooperative development process.

In More's words:

> Recent evidence provides numerous examples of technology based industrial product organizations having difficulty in profitably introducing new products into potential customer organizations. Adoption of these new products has frequently been much slower than expected, has provided lower profit margins, has required much greater developer resources than expected, and in some cases has resulted in withdrawal from the market with severe financial losses. These problems have been attributed by many observers to failure in effectively managing the development process, and in some cases this has support. In other cases, however, the real failure of managers in developing organizations has been in understanding and managing their strategic relationships with potential adopting organizations. In many of these situations, more effective management of these interorganizational relationships may have had a major impact on success in the situation. Several frameworks have been formulated to structure either the development process or the adop-

FIGURE 4–3.
Relationship Examples
RELATIONSHIP EXAMPLES

A. TRADITIONAL DEVELOPER-DRIVEN SERIAL RELATIONSHIP
B. ADOPTER-PROACTIVE CO-DEVELOPMENT RELATIONSHIP

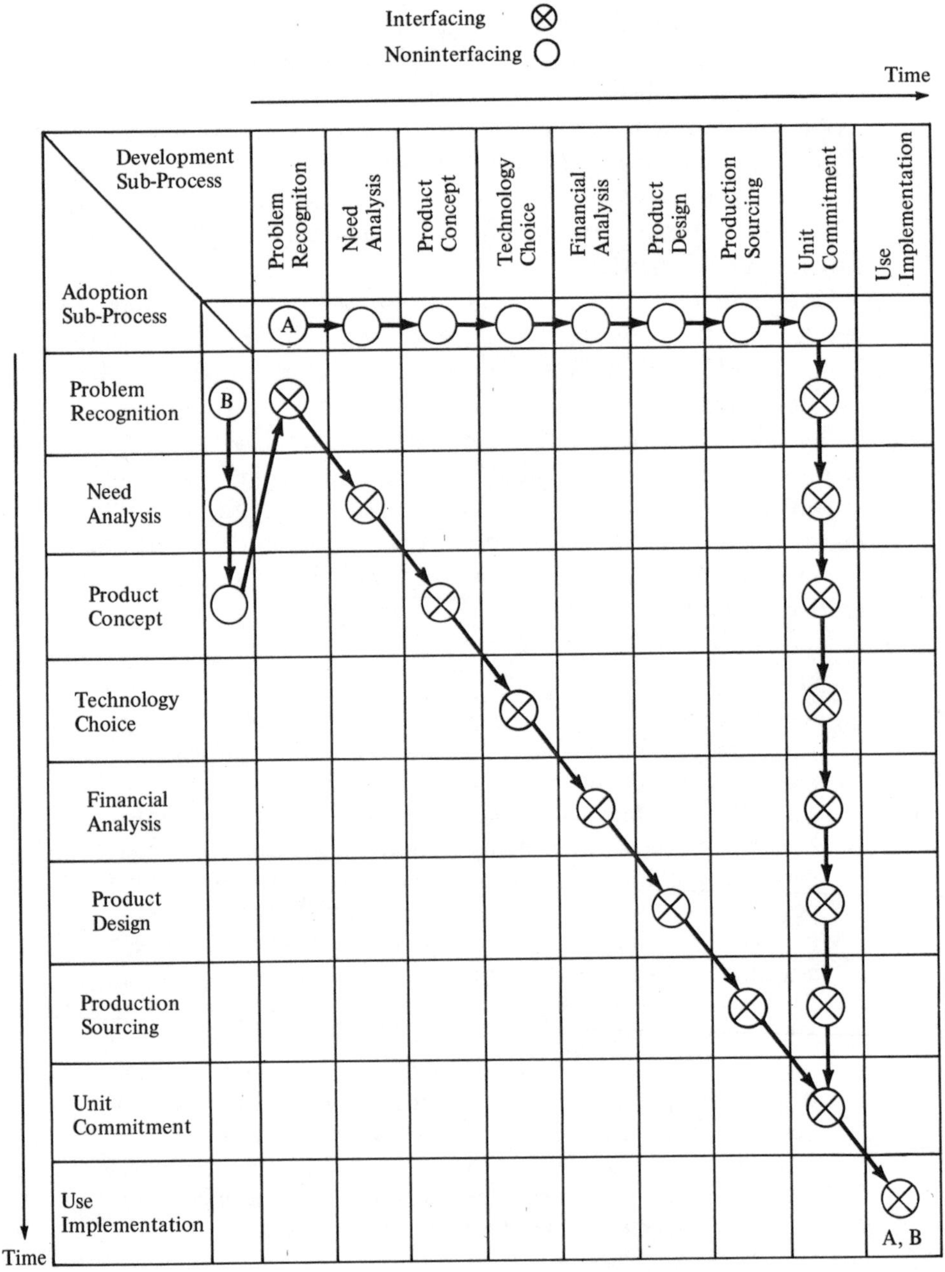

tion process. Few have been formulated which explicitly conceptualize alternative interorganizational relationships.[2]

Roger More developed a framework for conceptualizing and managing developer/adopter relationships. The framework breaks the process down into three subprocesses: the development subprocess, the adoption subprocess, and the interfacing subprocess. Using the framework, More shows examples of both a traditional supplier-driven relationship and the equivalent of what this text calls reverse marketing (see Figure 4–3). The framework integrates the three subprocesses to generate important strategic implications for managers of both supplier and purchasing organizations.

It is interesting that this industrial marketing research confirms the need for reverse marketing in technology-based situations and clearly identifies the difficulty in effectively managing this development.

BRIEF SUMMARY

1. Technology and reverse marketing are closely linked.

2. Either the purchaser's own technological progress and/or a supplier's new technology may cause a need for reverse marketing.

3. Even small purchasers can initiate technology-driven reverse marketing.

4. Technology-driven reverse marketing may have a major impact on an organization's competitive edge.

5. The risks of failure in technology-driven reverse marketing may be substantial for both sides and the liability of each party needs to be agreed to beforehand.

6. It may take a long time to develop a new technology.

7. The supplier's search in technology should be world-wide.

8. The quality of the communication link between purchaser and supplier is crucial.

9. The purchaser with sound common sense and an inquisitive nature can make a useful contribution even in highly sophisticated technological development. Extra resources, however, need to be available to supply the technological muscle.

10. Large suppliers are more likely to have the research strength and the financial resources to entertain a significant investment in a new technology.

11. A strong multifunctional effort will have to be mounted by the purchaser in any major reverse marketing effort that is technology driven.

Social, Political, and Environmental Concerns

THE idea that the supply function might contribute in a social or political way to the well-being of the organization was originally stoutly resisted by many purchasing practitioners. They saw their role as focusing on value (and value meant price). Bringing in different criteria for supplier selection just interfered with supply's perceived mission. Perhaps it is a sign of maturity of the function that in the past decade increasing attention has been paid to the social, political, and environmental dimensions of procurement policy. For example, the City of New York's purchasers insisted that only those suppliers that used recycled paper would be invited to bid. Military supply officers, for security reasons, often insist that domestically owned and domestically located suppliers be considered. In numerous countries, governmental purchasers have insisted that foreign suppliers meet minimum local content targets. In the United States, legislation requires the use of minority suppliers. In Canada, the federal government announced its intention to spread federal purchases across the country in percentages reflecting the population densities of the provinces. In some countries local preference laws stipulate a percentage by which a local supplier may exceed the price of a foreign competitor and still get the business. In many countries purchasers have become concerned about placing orders with suppliers who do not respect the environment.

Whether the push comes from legislation or "enlightened self-interest," the additional requirements of social, political, or environmental objectives to traditional value concerns have put additional pressure on purchasers to use reverse marketing.

The case Plastico Inc., which follows, illustrates some of the social and political parameters influencing successful reverse marketing.

CASE: PLASTICO INC.

The National Oceanic and Atmospheric Administration (NOAA) was continually exploring ways of making the nation's fishing industry more efficient. One of its current projects was the Inshore Fish Handling Program which addressed the whole process of fish handling from the time the fish were caught until they arrived at the packing plant for processing. The traditional method of fish handling, which had been used for generations, consisted of unloading the catch by hand from the boat into buggies by using pitchforks, wheeling them over to a small scale for weighing, then dumping the fish back onto the wharf. When an open stake-truck arrived with ice from the packing plant, the fish would be forked by hand into the truck. After the truck arrived at the plant, the fish were again forked onto the plant holding-room floor and re-iced prior to processing. This excess handling of the fish caused damage resulting in a lower quality product which financially affected both the fishermen and the fish processing firms.

The NOAA was therefore interested in discovering ways to improve the present outdated system of fish handling to make it more efficient and result in better quality fish.

During his ongoing search of the latest literature in the field, John Howe, the chief engineer in charge of the coastal region, realized that the containerization principle might be applicable to fish handling problems. Further investigation revealed that some Scandinavian countries had started to use containers in their fishing industries. Fish were put in a container with ice at dockside and were not handled again until they were ready to be processed at the plant.

Howe decided to obtain a sample of the fish containers used by other countries. After considerable effort he was able to import one and immediately began to study its applicability to the fish handling problem he was facing. At this point he reasoned that a full-scale in-use test was warranted and he went through the proper government channels to purchase 1000 standard containers of the appropriate size, but not designed for fish, from a local subsidiary of a large international plastics manufacturer. This local firm imported 300 units from its parent in another country and manufactured the remaining 700 locally to fill the order. The containers were subsequently loaned to fish plants which tested their use in comparison with the conventional methods and found the concept to be sound. This initial batch of containers, however, lacked sufficient durability and were damaged easily with the inevitable rough treatment they received. Also, several design features of the containers were not completely compatible with the new fish handling system that Howe wished to introduce.

By now Howe was convinced that the container principle had promise for his proposed system, but the initial field test showed that significant changes to the container would be required for satisfactory service.

He then contacted the General Services Administration (GSA), which handled procurement of this type for the federal government. In his initial discussions with Alex Wielund of the GSA, he explained the problems of using a product that was bulky to transport and whose existing design was not completely suited to his specific needs. Mr. Wielund sympathized with Howe and said: "It would certainly make life easier for you if we had a local supplier who could work with you to implement any necessary design changes and could produce them closer to the scene of your operations to minimize transportation costs. Also, the fisheries area is one of high unemployment and any new jobs created there would be welcome. It is a long-standing policy of our department to buy locally wherever economically feasible and to create jobs in slow-growth areas."

Wielund, who had many years of experience in all types of government procurement, realized that the technology to manufacture the required containers existed in the central part of the country but that there were no potential suppliers close to the scene of fisheries operations. In addition, apart from the domestic supplier for the initial container contract, there was no other domestic supplier with the tooling available to produce the required containers. The original producer was reluctant to entertain design changes, large or small, arising from the field trials of the container, because it already had customers in other industries satisfied with its current container.

Based on the results and experience of the field trials with the initial batch of containers, general drawings and specifications for an improved container were developed by the technical experts of the NOAA and the GSA. Since the NOAA required a large number of containers and forecast good prospects for future orders, all known domestic sources were solicited. All those interested were sent a request for a proposal, the key conditions of which, apart from price, delivery, and conformance to specifications, were:

1. a requirement to produce prototypes off production tooling for acceptance prior to commencement of production
2. the testing of prototypes under severe conditions equivalent to those found in the field
3. the establishment of a facility in the coastal region in which a significant number of containers were to be produced under the contract
4. the granting of royalty-free nonexclusive design rights, drawings, and specifications to the federal government for future bidding purposes.

Interested potential suppliers were also requested to review the information provided and then to meet with the NOAA officers six weeks before the proposal deadline to ensure that what was being requested was practical, feasible, and economical, to clarify any misunderstandings, and to exchange ideas on improving the process to the mutual benefit of suppliers and the government.

This meeting was attended by eight firms, and it produced a lively exchange of ideas. The request for proposals was subsequently "hardened" to include agreed-to ideas and changes.

At the deadline, four proposals—including one from the original supplier—were received. After extensive analysis, GSA procurement officers narrowed the list to two sources, not including the original supplier. The most interesting proposal, and also the one with the lowest submitted price—about $300 per container—was submitted by Plastico Inc. Plastico agreed to open a manufacturing facility in the coastal area and also expressed willingness to entertain design changes as the project progressed. This particularly appealed to John Howe, because he felt that the whole project was still evolving and that flexibility on the part of the manufacturer was important. After a two-month evaluation period, several visits to the Plastico Inc. plant, and much discussion with Jack Hebert, Plastico's president, Alex Wielund was convinced of Plastico's ability to produce the containers to the new and acceptable design. A contract for 7000 containers to be produced within a year was signed by both parties, with the stipulation that a substantial number of the containers be produced in a new plant in the coastal region.

At the beginning of the contract period, Plastico manufactured the containers at its main plant, which was not located in the fisheries area. Before the year was out, Plastico transferred the fish container production to its new leased plant in the coastal region, creating 24 jobs. It was found that Jack Hebert and his firm were highly innovative and interested in product improvement to meet the operational needs developing from field experience with his containers. The rapport between the firm and the government officials involved in the project was excellent. During this first year there were several design changes and, as set out in the contract, the cost of these changes was first negotiated with both parties. The vendor maintained that the negotiated prices for changes to the fish container did not cover all the costs and Plastico had to absorb some of them.

As the first year drew to a close and the 7000 containers were completed, a second contract was given to Plastico, this time for 3000 containers, a sole-source contract. There were still more design changes, and by the end of the second year the containers being produced were the fifth generation of the container specifications that had been laid down at the original information meeting almost three years earlier. By this time, Plastico Inc. had broadened its product line at the new plant to produce plastic fish buoys, floating docks, septic tanks, and small boats. This meant that the firm was now not solely dependent upon government business for its survival.

With each significant additional requirement for containers the GSA faced a problem: it was basic government policy to go to competition wherever reasonable and possible. The government had rights to the design of the container actually produced under the original contract but not to the subsequent design changes, some of considerable significance, developed by the firm in response to user experience. In addition, for operational reasons, the NOAA sent its requirements to other suppliers with insufficient lead time for these suppliers to acquire tooling, test, and produce containers in time to meet the required deliveries. Thus, after four years, a final sole-source contract for 4000 containers was awarded to Plastico on the clear understanding—agreed to by NOAA, the firm, and the GSA—that the next requirement would go to competition taking whatever lead time was necessary and fair. It was agreed that subsequent design changes would be handled in a manner that did not divulge the proprietary design solutions developed by Plastico.

When the next contract for 3000 containers was put out to bid, the competition was strong but Plastico won it on price.

Because Plastico had also developed other related products (e.g., buoys, docks, and boats), by the time of the third bidding round, its coastal plant's sales of fish containers amounted to only 5 percent of that plant's total output.

Plastico had proven itself not only by supplying an excellent product but also by surviving in a very competitive marketplace. The NOAA project had proven itself successful and acceptable to the industry. In addition, a small but viable industry had been established in an area of high unemployment.

REVERSE MARKETING INSIGHTS FROM THE PLASTICO EXPERIENCE

The experience of the two government agencies involved with Plastico in the fish container example highlights a number of social and political concerns that can surface during a reverse marketing program. These considerations may appear to work at cross purposes to commonly held reverse marketing objectives, as governmental reverse marketing initiatives may not be driven by the profit motive.

The initiative for reverse marketing in this instance came from one government department—the National Oceanic Atmospheric Administration (NOAA), which identified the need. Another government department—the General Services Administration (GSA)—carried out the actual reverse marketing. The final user of the fish containers—the fisheries industry—did not initiate the reverse marketing project. The ultimate objective was not to benefit any government department—they would not actually use the fish containers—but the fishing industry as a whole. The Plastico example presents the conflicting goals of two departments of the same government—the procurement agency (GSA) was anxious to be seen as utilizing fair procurement policies, whereas the user (NOAA) wanted a close and developmental relationship with a vendor, preferring a local vendor for easier communication. For a variety of reasons, the GSA did not pursue the original vendor which supplied the first 1000 containers.

The Plastico example shows that the process of engaging in reverse marketing differs somewhat when social and political objectives predominate.

The user agency (NOAA) saw the need and went to the supply agency (GSA) which then initiated the reverse marketing effort. The supply agency's initial efforts were unsatisfactory because they placed expediency in obtaining bids ahead of a thorough well-thought-out proposal by potential vendors. Surrounding the Plastico development was the government's desire to support overall government initiatives such as assisting a weak industry—fisheries, assisting employment in a high unemployment area, and regional development. The project, by its very nature, was developmental and experimental, with specification changes throughout its duration. Ownership of the specifications was supposed to stay with the government agency, not with Plastico, and Plastico was not happy about this. Apparently, the GSA did not fully recognize the evolutionary nature of the fish container design and ended up owning rights to the original design which quickly became obsolete as further changes were made.

A supplier switch had occurred early in the project when the original vendor was unwilling to work with government purchasers in altering its standard container design to suit the fishing industry's needs. This original vendor could not see enough long-term payoff to warrant being flexible in product design.

A hypothetical question can be raised regarding the selection of Plastico. Which supplier would have been selected had Plastico not submitted the lowest bid? For example, what if Plastico had been the only supplier willing to invest in a new plant in the coastal fisheries region, but was, at the same time, a higher bidder? As it was, the GSA did not have to face such a dilemma. Perhaps the work done in advance of the bidding round was instrumental in achieving the desirable result.

The changes in specifications and the related price negotiations tend to be unusual in most government contracts. Typical government contracts have predetermined specifications which are not frequently altered. In the Plastico example, fixed contracts were issued but changes were allowed—these were negotiated changes between both parties. The prices agreed to for the changes did not completely cover the vendor's costs for these changes. Had the government been willing to cover all the costs of the changes, it would have put itself in a preferred position to own the new specifications. In a sense, a degree of unfairness to the vendor might be seen to have crept in here because of the government's insistence that specifications be disclosed for future bidding by other suppliers.

The government was willing to participate in development with Plastico, share costs, and sole source with them, but hoped to retain design rights so the fish boxes could subsequently be put out to bid. One objective of the government purchasing agency was to get back to normal supply routines as soon as possible. In reality, it took four years to reach this point.

The user department and the vendor cooperated closely through the many specification changes. Also, the vendor's dependence on this government contract in the first two years was very high, because almost all production was geared to fish containers. Plastico recognized the need to diversify on its own. Its success in producing other products helped avoid a serious potential future dilemma for the GSA. What action would the GSA have taken if Plastico had remained exclusively a fish-container producing plant and had submitted a higher price on the last 3000 container order than a vendor located elsewhere?

Measures of Success

When political and social motives for reverse marketing predominate, measures of success may differ from those when the primary objective is solely to improve value. In the Plastico case the measures of success were: (1) NOAA obtained a new technology, (2) the federal government assisted in creating new jobs in a high unemployment region, (3) the fishing industry was able to receive higher quality fish, more product, less spoilage, and lower handling costs.

Unique Aspects of Governmental Reverse Marketing

Governmental agencies can engage in reverse marketing even though this appears to be contrary to the purchasing practice of acquisition by competitive bid. The notion of reverse marketing in public procurement seems to be contrary to the government's objective of being perceived to be equally fair to all suppliers. Reverse marketing, almost by definition, means giving preferential treatment to one supplier over others. Over a four-year period, Plastico was a sole source, and all fish container requirements were basically negotiated. There were a number of mitigating circumstances, however. The vendor had just established a new plant in a high unemployment area. The NOAA was trying to introduce a new fish handling method and wished to be seen by the fishermen as responsive to their needs. This, in turn, required frequent and rapid design changes to test alternate box designs. Thus, uncertainty regarding specifications and total requirements was high, preventing routine bid solicitation. Whether four years was an appropriate period to suspend competitive bidding was a judgement call. The ultimate user of the fish containers was not a governmental employee or a department but private industry. The project was unusual because originally the fish containers were a giveaway item. The two primary issues in the Plastico case were: (1) the government initiated the development, and (2) there were social concerns involved—jobs were created in a high unemployment area and assistance was given to a distressed industry. It is perfectly normal for a private organization to engage in reverse marketing for social and political reasons but the Plastico example happens to involve a government initiative, which adds some special dimensions.

The Plastico example did not involve just one government department but two—the initiator of the project (NOAA) was not the department (GSA) that implemented the development. The government was the only customer for the fish containers, and there were no guarantees to Plastico that any further orders for these containers would be forthcoming even after the plant was constructed in the coastal region.

The Plastico example presents a delicate straddle between traditional government concerns for adherence to policies and procedures (i.e., lowest cost option determined through the bidding route) versus the social/political concerns given the reality of the situation. The most economical fish container could probably have been manufactured at Plastico's original plant, yet a new plant was constructed in a high unemployment coastal region. Traditional purchasing procedures were overridden by these political objectives.

In addition to the specific issues raised above in the Plastico case, other social and political issues may also give rise to reverse marketing. Some of these are illustrated below.

Another initiative involving "political" overtones was demonstrated by a federal governmental agency responsible for the sale and control of government bonds and currency. The department had only two suppliers of security printing (involving steel engraving of latent images as a security feature), and production could be jeopardized if a strike at one supplier spread to the other, since both firms had the same union. To alleviate the problem, the federal agency worked with a third printer (nonunion) that already had obtained the required security clearance and possessed the expertise and capability but did not have the proper steel press equipment to compete with the existing suppliers. However, because of the nature of government bidding, no guarantee of future contracts could be given and this third printer had to be competitive with other qualified suppliers. Although the purchaser wanted a third supplier, one that was nonunion to give a message to its union suppliers, no favoritism could be given to the developed supplier.

REVERSE MARKETING AND MINORITY SUPPLIERS

Working to develop solid sources of supply with minority firms which initially have very little potential has both altruistic and legislated overtones. Many firms wish to demonstrate that they are good corporate citizens; moreover, U.S. Public Law 95-507 lays down specific requirements in dealing with minority suppliers for prime government contractors.

Research by Giunipero[1] has addressed the minority supplier issue and given several insights into the development of such suppliers and developed guidelines in the development of a stable, long-term relationship. The research found that purchasing problems encountered with minority suppliers are often quite different from those faced with nonminority suppliers. In particular, significant difficulties were experienced in locating minority businesses and identifying those with sufficient technical management skills. The areas of greatest difference between minority and nonminority groups were found to be: (1) lack of qualified engineering personnel, (2) lack of qualified sales personnel, (3) insufficient technological expertise. Three other common problem areas when dealing with minority vendors were found to be: (1) lack of minority vendors at or near operating locations, (2) lack of minority vendors supplying items required, and (3) minority vendors serving as fronts for nonminority businesses.

The relevant issue is how reverse marketing can be most helpful in assisting minority firms in becoming viable long-term suppliers. The research by Guinipero put forth a number of reverse marketing ideas which proved successful when tailored toward minority vendors:

1. Actively seek and initiate contacts with vendors
2. Use external directories which list minority vendors
3. Attend minority trade fairs
4. Obtain membership in a national or regional minority purchasing council
5. Provide technical assistance to minority vendors, including quality control and engineering assistance
6. Break larger purchases into quantities easily handled by a minority vendor
7. Help minority vendors develop effective purchasing practices
8. Assist minority vendors in securing raw materials
9. Be willing to pay a price differential
10. Provide management assistance.

The Raytheon Experience

The Raytheon Corporation, a high-tech multinational with more than 64,000 employees and world-wide sales in excess of $3 billion, embarked on a minority reverse marketing program six years before Public Law 95-507 was passed in 1978. Raytheon's number of minority vendors has increased from 36 to 325 since the program's inception.

Raytheon subscribes to the "set aside" principle for a broad list of recurring company needs (e.g., packaging tapes, lumber). Part of these basic needs are "set aside" or earmarked for minority suppliers for two reasons: (1) minority suppliers are given a chance to supply on a wide variety of items, (2) minority suppliers are prevented from committing themselves to supply too large a quantity, i.e., all Raytheon's requirements.

Raytheon provides a professional consulting service to minority vendors. The firm also uses the services of its retired executives as volunteer consultants to assist minority suppliers in many facets of running a successful business and becoming a better supplier to Raytheon.

Often if a minority supplier can show a bank that it has a contract with Raytheon, then the bank will advance it a line of credit. A small supplier (minority or not) frequently needs more business than just the Raytheon contract to keep the particular machine(s) in the plant busy. The supplier is often unaware of other potential customers or lacks the resources to develop them. Raytheon has aided these suppliers in meeting the right buyers in potential customer firms and has assisted them in soliciting additional business. Raytheon will do marketing research for the minority and/or small supplier to identify where the supplier should go for additional business.

The Detroit Edison Company

The Detroit Edison Company is an investor-owned utility supplying electric power to customers in a 7600 square mile area of southeastern Michigan. More than 15 percent of its individual power customers are members of minority groups. Detroit Edison wanted to foster business practices that would promote a more stable and secure Michigan and Detroit, in light of the city's history of race relations.

In an effort to achieve these ends, a nonprofit organization, the Economic Development Corporation (EDC) was formed in Detroit, under the auspices of 15 of the city's largest firms, to aid the growth of minority business locally. To assist in realizing this objective, a subdivision of EDC, called the Industrial Purchasing Committee (IPC), consisting of the heads of purchasing of the 15 EDC members, was formed. It was reasoned that the large corporations had to provide leadership and perhaps take risks that the smaller organizations could not.

In addition to Detroit Edison's active participation in EDC and IPC, the firm's purchasing department made a special effort to obtain as much information on minority suppliers as possible from publications and by being in direct contact with purchasing people within EDC and outside as well. Detroit Edison also set an annual targeted dollar amount to be sourced with minority vendors.

Raytheon and Detroit Edison are only two of many firms that have successfully developed minority suppliers.

The Bixton Example

In another example, a large computer firm, Bixton, was awarded a large government contract for systems hardware. The contract called for 100 percent local content plus industrial and regional benefits—all of which had to be documented. The problem faced by the firm's purchasing department was to find and develop suppliers in depressed areas to furnish state-of-the-art technology that would meet military standards of quality assurance. A countrywide search was conducted for small, minority suppliers in all of the business areas needed for the project. The objective was to locate those with the potential to be developed into viable suppliers. Those so identified were approached with an explanation of the requirements, responsibilities, obligations, and potential rewards. To accomplish this, Bixton set up a special development or "persuasion" team which consisted of manufacturing, logistics, quality, and financial experts. This team worked with the local suppliers as they made the transition to becoming first-rate suppliers.

Common Threads in Minority Reverse Marketing

Listed below are some common elements of which the purchaser should be cognizant when concerned with enlisting and developing minority supply sources:

1. Typically, minority suppliers are undercapitalized and a firm supply contract with a large firm can often assist them in obtaining more financing.

2. Minority suppliers often need assistance in technical matters, hands-on assistance, and help in obtaining financing. When assistance is offered, the supplier is often hard to convince that the offer of assistance is genuine; the question "What's the catch?" is often heard.

3. Many minority suppliers underestimate the complexity of supplying to a large, technically advanced firm.

4. Minority suppliers are typically inadequately equipped in marketing—they don't know the right questions to ask of a particular customer.

5. Minority suppliers who subsequently became good supply sources all had something they were good at, but often the basic management principles were lacking.

6. It is often necessary to get the confidence of minority suppliers before they will disclose details of their real capabilities.

7. Some minority suppliers refuse assistance and may be intimidated by a large firm offering assistance.

8. It is key to be able to identify where problems will likely occur in developing a particular minority supplier.

9. Dealing with minority suppliers can make buyers better business people by forcing them to think things through and anticipate many possible eventualities. Also, many of the reverse marketing techniques used with minority suppliers can be applied to their general purchasing functions.

DEVELOPING NONPROFIT ORGANIZATIONS AS SOURCES OF SUPPLY

In some instances it is possible to develop supply sources with organizations whose existence is based on social objectives alone. An example will illustrate this point.

The Chelmsford Toy Company, a well-known manufacturer of a wide variety of quality toys, was evaluating alternative methods of packaging some of its toy lines. The firm wanted to move to blister-pack packaging from a currently used less-than-satisfactory method.

The alternatives open to Chelmsford included purchasing the blister-pack equipment and having its own employees do the packaging, contracting the job out to a custom packaging house, or working with a social agency which ran a number of sheltered workshops to develop this as a source of packaging expertise.

The sheltered workshop agency was under pressure from its funding agency, The United Way, to generate more revenue through its business division and thus was anxious to perform the packaging work for Chelmsford.

The quotation received from the workshop was the best submitted from potential packaging suppliers, but certain issues were raised by Chelmsford management, such as the effect on their current suppliers if Chelmsford developed the sheltered workshop as a supply source and whether Chelmsford would have to supply quality control to the workshop.

The Chelmsford example raises an interesting issue: to what extent should a purchaser try to go to develop a source of supply that is governed by nonprofit motives. In accepting the workshop's quotation, the firm had to accept the reality that the sheltered workshop would probably require greater initial assistance to get it on stream than a regular supplier and perhaps a different arrangement for quality assurance. In addition, Chelmsford's regular suppliers might view this source with suspicion since the social agency, supported in part by public funds, could be competitive with services offered because its costs were subsidized and it was not truly profit oriented. The purchaser also had to be aware that a lower price quoted by a sheltered workshop could be the result of exploitation of its workforce,[2] a practice with which the purchasing firm would not want to be associated. Care had to be taken that the lower wages paid to workers in the sheltered workshop reflected lower productivity rather than exploitation of the workers.

In another sheltered workshop development initiative, top management in a firm challenged purchasing to place some work with sheltered workshops as a good corporate citizen gesture. Purchasing's first step was to identify the areas in the manufacturing process that lent themselves to a sheltered workshop environment, which turned out to be sorting and packing. The initial year's experience showed the firm that the sheltered workshop was capable of handling much more than routine sorting and packing. Through numerous meetings with the workshop's supervisory personnel, added challenges were given to the employees resulting in skill development and increasing work abilities. The result was a new supplier for the firm, an enhanced good corporate citizen image in the community and a better trained workforce at the sheltered workshop.

LOCAL CONTENT REQUIREMENTS

Governments at all levels—municipal, regional, state, or federal—almost without exception have as one of their objectives the nurturing and development of local industry and the attendant increase in employment. The influence exerted by the various governmental levels takes many different forms, from an encouragement to buy locally, to paying a premium for local purchases, to enacting local content legislation. These realities impact on many firms' selling policies in that one of the conditions of having access to a lucrative market might well be developing a substantial supply source in that market. The following examples illustrate some of the ramifications of local content requirements on reverse marketing.

Initially assisted in gaining global recognition by U.S. Navy Seabees who left their Caterpillar equipment in foreign countries after World War II, the Caterpillar Tractor Company[3] is considered to be a world-class global firm with assembly plants in each of its major markets—Europe, Japan, Brazil, Australia, and the United States. In all instances, Caterpillar has become heavily involved in the local economy. In sourcing locally, the firm has achieved lower costs, retained local product flexibility, and become a friend rather than a threat to local governments.

Another global company, farm equipment manufacturer Varity Corporation Ltd.,[4] is often coerced by developing countries into opening plants and sourcing locally if it wishes to do business in those countries. Even though Varity could save a third-world country money by supplying tractors produced in one world-scale plant in England or Brazil, saving money is not always the first priority of an image-conscious government.

Libya insisted on Varity opening a tractor plant and sourcing locally, although the country had no real need for one. Iran, under the late Shah, insisted on having a fully integrated tractor plant although the local economy was only proficient at providing relatively simple components and was unable to produce higher technology ones.

The McDonnell-Douglas Corporation of Los Angeles in 1980[5]

was awarded a long-term contract by the Canadian government for 137 F-18A fighter aircraft with a total estimated value of $4 billion. The cost of the planes would be $2.4 billion with the remainder being spent on missiles, logistical support, and spare parts. One of the prime criteria of the Canadian government in selecting the winning bid was the distribution of industrial benefits of the contract to Canadian suppliers. The McDonnell-Douglas commitment provided about 70,000 person-years of work in Canada over the life of the contract—equivalent to 4000 permanent jobs.

In preparation for its bid, McDonnell-Douglas sent teams of purchasers to Canada to investigate the feasibility of sourcing locally. Team members frequently found themselves in the reverse marketing mode to persuade potential vendors of the need to quote aggressively, so that McDonnell-Douglas could be competitive in its bid.

The awarding of this contract to McDonnell-Douglas over its world-class rivals emphasized its commitment to source and create jobs in Canada, which apparently gave it the winning edge over the competition.

In another example, a company was awarded a contract to construct a portion of the Alaska Highway Gas Pipe Line on condition that local content rules be followed to mazimize long-term local industrial benefits. The primary problem was a lack of local suppliers with enough expertise. A proven Italian firm was convinced to set up a local fitting plant to be a prime supplier of parts formerly sourced in Italy. Quality from the new operation was found to be lacking, resulting in the loan of specialists by the major contract holder. The result: a fitting manufacturer emerged employing over 100 people producing a quality product at a competitive price. Rather than having a need which couldn't be filled, reverse marketing was utilized to promote regional economic benefits.

In conducting reverse marketing for social, political, and environmental reasons, ultimately the difficulty lies in dealing with the trade-offs between relatively easily measured economic value versus the "softer" concerns which may be far more difficult to measure. In the final analysis the purchaser may not be the best person to make the decision but may have to present alternatives to other people in the organization who may have different perspectives on the issues involved.

In cases where a premium in price needs to be paid to achieve a social, political, or environmental objective, the purchaser may have no choice but to pass the decision to the appropriate decision maker in the organization, pointing out the premium involved. It is noteworthy, however, that with reverse marketing it may not at all be necessary to start from the premise that good economic value needs to be sacrificed to achieve social, political, or environmental objectives. In fact, it may be possible to achieve the best of both worlds, good economic *and* good other value.

BRIEF SUMMARY

1. Social, political, and environmental objectives may create a need for reverse marketing.

2. It is difficult to assess trade-offs between social, political, and environmental concerns and more traditional value components such as quality, delivery, price, and service.

3. In minority sourcing reverse marketing is almost essential.

4. Local content rules favor the use of reverse marketing.

5. Public organizations can engage in reverse marketing but this conflicts with the competitive bidding process. In governmental procurement reverse marketing can be used to bring suppliers to the point where they can compete successfully in the normal competitive bidding process.

6. It may not be necessary to pay a higher price, or to forego quality, delivery, and/or service objectives to achieve social, political, and environmental objectives. With reverse marketing it may be possible to achieve all objectives without compromise.

CHAPTER 6

Supply Trends and Reverse Marketing

SIGNIFICANT changes are taking place in the whole field of supply, many of which reinforce the need for further emphasis on reverse marketing. Major trends congruent with reverse marketing include a greater emphasis on quality, material requirements planning (MRP), just-in-time delivery, learning curve, computerization and greater exploitation of communications technology, systems contracting, longer-term contracts, continuing improvement and more single sourcing. Global companies have special needs for reverse marketing and the experience of Japanese companies in and outside of Japan provide further reinforcement in this chapter.

QUALITY

Achievement of high quality standards has traditionally received perfunctory attention in many areas of materials management. Increased international competition and the growing recognition of the high cost of unacceptable quality have, fortunately, pushed quality into the limelight. It is no longer possible simply to pay lip service to the need for high quality. Purchasers now demand the hard proof that current standards are being met and that even tighter future standards are set as new targets to be achieved. This belated awakening to the importance of quality has spawned the need for a tremendous amount of education of purchasers and suppliers alike. The understanding and effective use of statistical quality control concepts and techniques require extensive education of personnel in a wide variety of functions. The need for continuing improvement in quality performance has also required a major philosophical readjustment of workers and managers alike. The traditional view that a reasonable number of defects was to be accepted, since better quality performance would be more costly, was successfully challenged by such authors as Deming[1] and Crosby.[2] According to Deming, the supplier producing more defects must be the higher-cost supplier, because the cost of those defects is added to the total cost of production. In his book *Quality Is Free,* Crosby challenged the old myth that perfect quality is too expensive and proved it need not be so. This new perspective on quality holds a special challenge for the purchaser. Quality has become a more important procurement objective, but has also required a degree of purchaser-vendor collaboration which extends well beyond the negotiation table. Not only is it necessary for the purchaser's organization to get its own house in order, but it must persuade the vendor to do likewise. Frequently, simple acceptance of this need by the vendor is not sufficient; the vendor lacks the means and the drive to see it through. Moreover, it may be necessary to go beyond the first-line vendors themselves. Frequently, their quality difficulties stem from *their* suppliers and so on. Thus, a purchasing organization seriously interested in achieving significant long-term quality improvement is called upon to start a program of supplier selection, education, and support of substantial proportions. In our simple language this is a major reverse marketing challenge.

Signetics Electronics' Experience

The short description of the program followed by Signetics, a high-technology manufacturer, to bring its suppliers up to speed on quality standards is typical of the kind of effort that may be required and the length of time to achieve it. The cost of such efforts may well be considerable, reinforcing Deming's argument that high-quality suppliers are hard to find and should be highly preferred over others.

> Phase I is complete when Signetics and the vendor agree on inspection measurement procedures and techniques. There is also

mutual agreement that inspection of the same product leads to exact correlation. Every supplier completing Phase I is awarded a Certificate of Certification.

During Phase I, the labeling, packaging, transportation, and billing of shipment samples is agreed on. In addition, agreement is also reached on the frequency of maintaining correlation between inspectors and calibration of inspection equipment.

A control chart is developed for each inspection measurement. An upper and lower limit is also established based on equipment and inspection tolerances and differences. The data received from the vendor and the data generated by Signetics must fall within the established percentage of uncertainty. Reasons for any deviations are determined and corrections are made accordingly.

Phase II begins with a material conformance control analysis. This is accomplished by using additional correlation samples. For each measurement taken, control charts track the vendor's performance to specification. When a vendor exhibits consistent control of material conformance for a three-month period, he proceeds into Phase III.

In Phase III the vendor pulls all samples and does a complete outgoing inspection analysis. At Signetics' discretion these samples are used, either in part or in total, to dispose of the incoming shipment. A vendor who demonstrates that his quality history and inspection and process certification are in control for a three-month period will move into Phase IV.

Phase IV is the same as Phase III except samples and data are sent ahead of the shipment. This allows Signetics' Internal Quality Control (IQC) to operate in an audit mode by using vendor samples and data for preshipment or skip lot inspection. In this phase, the certified vendor supplies certification control samples/data, complete lot inspection samples/data, and a certificate of compliance. Shipments that are skipped have the supplied samples/data and certificate of compliance reviewed for inspection correlation and material conformance. No additional samples are inspected if all are found acceptable.

Continuous monitoring and auditing of Phases I–IV are the responsibility of Signetics IQC. Nonconformance issues and/or inspection correlation problems result in immediate stoppage of the program. Reinstitution occurs when all issues are resolved. . . .

The vendor communications program permits and encourages open lines of communication between Signetics and all suppliers. Driven by the purchasing department, the program provides reports and graphs to accurately track vendor quality performance. Each month, suppliers receive information including:

Performance summary data—lot acceptance rates, parts per million defective information, and defect mode analysis

Percent defective data for each inspected criterion

Lot acceptance rate/volume/PPM charts, and inspection correlation control charts, and

Vendor certification graphs.[3]

MRP AND JIT

The need for greater productivity and cost effectiveness has not only spurred the quality improvement drive, but also the efforts to reduce inventories and improve delivery control. Two popular concepts, material requirements planning (MRP) and just-in-time (JIT), both address inventory reduction and tight deliveries, although in different ways. MRP is computer dependent, using the distinction between dependent and independent demand and material explosion to built up schedules and to plan deliveries. Just-in-time production and inventory management in its pure form relies more heavily on industrial engineering and an experimental approach to inventory reduction. Clearly, both can be used in conjunction with one another, both require a substantial amount of reverse marketing. Extensive programs to discipline the purchaser's organization and vendors and their suppliers in turn are required to achieve long-term success.

One example of the start of such an effort is detailed in the following description of how General Motors in Canada worked with suppliers to implement the just-in-time philosophy. The firm's strategy was to implement the JIT concept and its basic principles gradually to increase its probability of success. A major step in obtaining supplier confidence and increasing two-way communication was the formation of the Suppliers' Council.

Suppliers' Council

The concept of the Suppliers' Council was discussed at the corporate level in General Motors United States through the firm's "Purchasing Congress" which is held four times a year. The congress, being unsure of how to activate the JIT concept, suggested that perhaps the Canadian General Motors operation could try to implement it.

In Canada, GM appointed 23 long-term suppliers from a supplier base of 800 to its newly formed Suppliers' Council. The 23 members represented a cross-section of commodity groups, geographic areas, size, and high dollar value and low dollar value parts. Also attending Council meetings, although not formally part of it, were a number of General Motors people from purchasing, quality control, and other materials areas.

The mission statement of the Council explains its primary purpose as one of information exchange, achieved through a two-way process.

The Council meets four times a year on GM premises with GM's Director of Purchasing acting as chairman. Council members are appointed by GM and serve a three-year term with one-third replaced each year. All administrative expenses are covered by GM which hosts a dinner after the all-day Council meetings. The suppliers are responsible for their own transportation and accommodation expenses.

In some instances, competing firms sit on the Council but this is not the rule. At the Council's onset, GM conducted a survey to obtain comments and suggestions concerning suppliers' relationships with GM. Some of the recommendations were:

1. Suppliers with purchased computer terminals (CRTs) that were on-line to GM wanted access to GM's daily "newsline," containing corporate news briefs which were available only to GM personnel. (Prior to setting up the Suppliers' Council, GM had installed CRTs and several suppliers became on-line to GM's production scheduling information).
2. Suppliers wanted more information on GM's scheduling system. The survey also revealed that those suppliers with CRTs liked them and preferred General Motors Canada's model year overlap system to that used by General Motors in the U.S.
3. Suppliers asked GM to expand the four-week flexible and five-day fixed production schedule to a four-week fixed one.
4. In the past, suppliers felt that there had been insufficient notice given of plant shutdowns and asked for more lead time of shutdowns. They cited cases of reading about forth-

coming shutdowns in the newspaper before hearing it from GM.
5. Suppliers noted that a slower mail service in Canada caused delay in receiving their weekly production schedules which were mailed by GM.

The Council's main activities have consisted of position papers presented by suppliers to GM and presentations by GM to the Council on specific topics of mutual concern. The main change since the Council was formed is that suppliers now feel GM does care about their welfare and that two-way dialogue has been facilitated. The Council is perceived by all suppliers as an impartial conduit to get messages or particular points of view across to GM. All suppliers now want to be part of the Council and it is considered a compliment to be asked to serve on it. Nonmembers have the perception that Council members are an "in group" with GM.

At the time of its formation, the Suppliers' Council at General Motors Canada was unique in North America, but purchasing management expected the concept to spread to General Motors in the United States and to the rest of the North American auto industry.

Since the initiation of the JIT program at GM, the level and nature of supplier assistance has changed. GM now has a full-time person traveling to suppliers to assist them in going on-line with General Motors and to handle communication problems. There are now product development teams going out to suppliers to help solve quality problems. These teams will hold meetings at suppliers' plants with supplier management and shop-floor workers attending. Also, supplier shop-floor workers are invited to visit the GM assembly plants to see how their part(s) fit into the vehicles being assembled.

GM uses the Source Performance Evaluation and Reporting (SPEAR) system of supplier evaluation to rate them on a five-point scale from 1 (excellent) to 5 (poor). GM's evaluators give suppliers their rating based on criteria such as delivery, and whether the supplier has statistical process control (SPC). Suppliers do not learn the SPEAR ratings of their competitors, but they are given a number for their own supplier quality index (SQI) and the average for their commodity group, which enables each supplier to compare its performance with the group as a whole.

Suppliers serious about improving their SPEAR rating are asked to submit an action plan to GM. If the plan is approved, GM will actively assist the supplier in making improvements. GM's SPEAR representatives, who used to visit suppliers as monitors, now go as consultants. "Package" supplier improvement programs are not used; each case is assessed individually and GM's assistance is tailored to the specific needs of the supplier.

With the adoption of the JIT philosophy, GM's involvement with suppliers has increased greatly. Functional areas such as engineering, quality control, and others from the materials control area as well as purchasing, are now more involved with suppliers. Whereas supplier liaison has always existed, it is much more prevalent now.

The JIT movement has meant internal changes in the purchasing and materials management functions at General Motors. Many in-house training programs such as those on SPC and quality control have been undertaken.

Significant supplier change is evident with adoption of the JIT philosophy. Many suppliers have accepted the challenge of better quality, delivery, and production efficiencies and have been successful, becoming more aggressive at the same time.

The GM example shows it is possible, and may be even necessary, to work with vendors both singly and in groups when all are challenged by a common goal such as JIT or quality improvement.

Implications of Just-in-Time for the Procurement Function

Adoption of the just-in-time concept results in major changes for the procurement function. Single sourcing of components is accompanied by long-term stable supplier relationships. Buying from vendors in close proximity who can deliver frequently and in small lots impacts upon the traffic function. Both buyer and supplier reap benefits through lower inventories, higher productivity, lower material costs, and higher quality.

Schonberger and Gilbert[4] examined the impact of just-in-time on the role of the procurement function and describe the concept's challenge for U.S. industry in the following ways:

1. "Suppliers develop a competency that is particularly attuned to the delivery and quality needs of the buying firm."

2. "The ideal in the Japanese view of JIT purchasing is zero buffer inventory via one-at-a-time continuous delivery from supplier to user."
3. "Basic duties of locating good suppliers, arranging agreements, and following up to assure compliance are still present."
4. Although it is not uncommon in the United States for buyers to perform a small amount of "missionary work" before placing an order, much more preliminary work is necessary under the JIT concept.
5. Benefits accrue to the suppliers—"benefits of long-term contracts, stable relationships with the buying plant, plus the potential to share peak capacity."
6. "JIT purchasing is facilitated by buying from a small number of nearby suppliers."
7. Buyers encourage and facilitate suppliers to locate near them.

Schonberger and Gilbert also identify the need for focused factories, designed to produce a narrow range of products at exact shipping quantities.

THE LEARNING CURVE OR MANUFACTURING PROCESS FUNCTION

The learning curve concept, originally reserved for military procurement and heavily focused on the aircraft industry, is gaining greater attention. It also has larger implications for reverse marketing. Texas Instruments, for example, uses it as a way of setting longer-term targets for itself and its suppliers. The argument goes like this. "We are a company in a highly competitive environment. For us to survive and prosper we need to be able to bring our long-term costs down significantly as fast as we can. To the best of our knowledge, in view of increasing volume and technological and other improvements it should be possible for you to achieve the following targets for the next three years. Should you agree, we are counting on you to achieve these targets. We are willing to assist you in a variety of ways to make sure you will achieve this. However, if you do not believe you can meet our future objectives, there is no point in making a deal with us now, even though you may be fully competitive now.''

The combination of a progressively tougher set of objectives with a longer contract term reinforces the need for reverse marketing. The difficulties of setting fair and equitable goals should not be minimized. Achieving these objectives becomes an even more difficult challenge for both purchaser and supplier. It is just not good enough for either side to bang their fists on the table and insist that something is possible or is not. Both sides need to work together to make sure that these progressive improvements become a reality.

COMPUTERIZATION AND COMMUNICATIONS TECHNOLOGY

The developments in computerization and communications technology, even when not combined, have already had a major impact on the management and execution of the whole logistics function. Their effective combination still offers massive opportunities for major changes in thinking about the field of materials management and how different objectives can be accomplished. Whereas the supply function has traditionally been seen as involving a tremendous amount of paperwork, much of this has already changed, and substantial improvements are still to come. The hook-up of the purchaser's computer to those of its suppliers and the sharing of common data bases are not just a matter of flicking the appropriate switches. A substantial amount of reverse marketing work has to precede the intertwining of networks. And the purchaser and supplier alike need to develop a healthy dose of trust in each other and each other's systems before such linking becomes an effective reality. The simple example of GM's Suppliers' Council in Canada where 23 of its preferred suppliers requested access to information routinely distributed to all GM employees is a good indication of the obstacle to be overcome. When purchasing relayed this request to others in GM, there was opposition to this idea at first. One can just imagine what requests for more sensitive information might face!

SYSTEMS CONTRACTING AND SYSTEMS PURCHASES

The popularity of such well-established concepts as systems contracting shows that with the appropriate amount of cooperation from both vendor and purchaser, both sides can end up winners. In a typical systems contract, the buyer and supplier decide on a catalog of items and prices and on delivery terms. Approved requisitioners can then place orders directly with the supplier and expect rapid delivery. The supplier bills bimonthly or monthly and also provides a computer printout listing all purchases over the period. Typical requirements covered by a systems contract include office, electrical, and plumbing supplies. Obviously, systems contracting itself can still benefit from a number of the new developments in communications technology. The idea of moving from the procurement of specific services, items, or commodities to the purchase of systems is not new and has already been accepted.

Current experiments by a number of companies have already proven some of the opportunities inherent in computerization and new communications technology. It appears that the major obstacles are likely to be human rather than technological. It looks as if there's a tremendous reverse marketing challenge ahead to exploit effectively the opportunities offered by new developments in computerization and new communications technology.

LONGER-TERM CONTRACTS AND SINGLE SOURCING

Almost all of the preceding examples in this chapter point to the need for a longer time horizon than that traditionally employed in the field of procurement. Improved quality, delivery, cost, flexibility, learning curve, computerization and communications systems all require reverse marketing to achieve results. They also require time. When the minimum time to bring a supplier to acceptable quality standards at a firm such as Signetics is two years (assuming no hitches at all along the way), it does not make much sense to talk in terms of six-month or one-year contracts. It is not just the cost of bringing both the purchaser's and supplier's organizations to peak levels of performance. This cost in itself argues that a return on their investment must be achieved, and such return can only come over time. Presumably also, the longer term is the carrot that needs to be held out to achieve the results requested. It would be silly for a purchaser to march into a vendor's premises and say: "I have some specific requirements that you can fulfill if you really are willing to put a massive effort behind it. I am going to ask you to rethink completely the way you are organized and how you manage, manufacture, inventory, schedule, and account for quality and delivery. And as soon as you can do all of these things well, I am not going to promise you any more business."

Of course, that doesn't make any sense. The ending line has to be "and if you can achieve what we need, I can promise you that we'll both have a good future together."

The most basic requirement of a really good supplier is that this supplier will worry about the present and future needs of the purchaser and how the supplier can help the purchaser improve, whether the purchaser demands it or not. And this brings on the question of single sourcing.

Single Sourcing

Traditional procurement wisdom has been that multiple sourcing increased the security of supply. Strikes, mishaps, quality problems, delivery interruptions, and the like which befall one supplier may not affect another. Hence, having at least two sources for critical supply items is sound practice.

Not so, argues Deming.[5] It is difficult enough to bring one supplier's quality up to desired levels; trying to do this for two sources just compounds the likelihood of failure and quality problems. It does make good procurement sense to hang on to an outstanding supplier. The traditional procurement problem has been finding outstanding suppliers. And hanging on to mediocre suppliers or switching mediocre suppliers frequently are both options of low appeal. As long as purchasers depended on competition almost exclusively to find outstanding suppliers, they were often disappointed. The more obvious solution: reverse marketing. If single sourcing makes more sense because of all of the trends in the procurement field mentioned earlier, it also requires a more active approach to create an outstanding supplier. Changing from multiple sources to a single source without changing the way the purchaser and supplier interact will lead to disappointment. Single sourcing with a mediocre supplier will produce mediocre results. Single sourcing should follow once suppliers, through their actual performance, have proven they can be reliable, high quality producers. Unfortunately, it is much easier to change from multiple sources to a single source than to create outstanding suppliers. Multiple sourcing is an admission that outstanding sources are not available. Hence, climbing on the bandwagon of single sourcing without putting forth the effort to create outstanding sources will produce nothing but disappointment.

GLOBAL COMPANIES' APPROACH TO REVERSE MARKETING

Global companies are now recognized as being a leading force in world business and evidence shows them as the winners in international competition. Characteristically, global comanies view the world as one market, are not constrained by national boundaries, and utilize integrated global strategies to their advantage. They perceive competition as global and formalize strategy on an integrated world-wide basis.

In the first instance, by its very nature, the global company typically views the world as its market for selling its products, to source materials and components, and in looking for production sites. It is normal for global companies to receive government pressure and intervention by countries seeking both capital investment and purchase commitments. This is particularly evident in developing countries and soft currency areas which compete among themselves to attract larger commitments from global companies.

From the global company's perspective, although supply market differences are recognized, risk decisions become more complex as the number of countries in which the company operates increases. The attempt to reduce risk in reverse marketing decisions often results in more headquarters' involvement.

In addressing the issue of reverse marketing and supply problems in developing countries, Farmer[6] cites areas of common concern:

1. Lack of technological back-up
2. Licence and foreign exchange difficulties

3. Poor service from indigenous supply sources (e.g., poor delivery schedule performance, quality failure, limited variety, etc.)
4. Political instability or risk, affecting investment (either with respect to the company itself or potential suppliers)
5. Tariffs and host government pressure to buy within the country
6. Governmental pressures regarding their own purchasing from the company
7. Necessity for carrying higher inventories
8. Necessity for intensifying goods inwards inspection activity
9. "Home" derived specifications not available from local supply markets
10. Quality inconsistency with certain imported components
11. Lack of trained local staff, affecting supply department performance

Even though the initial impetus for global companies' reverse marketing may be very diverse—from firm initiated to host country government initiated—Farmer draws several conclusions with respect to global reverse marketing efforts[7]:

1. Recognize that each location has a different environment.
2. Work to improve forecasting skills and sources of intelligence about pending political/economic/sociological changes in company-world supply markets.
3. Analyze and consider (1) supply markets, (2) process methodology, (3) make or buy, and (4) political/economic/sociological implications very carefully *prior* to making a plant location decision.
4. Work toward a policy of corporate involvement when and where necessary to achieve company-world objectives.
5. Ensure adequate capability and organization to meet specific needs in all company locations.
6. Recognize the entrepreneurial role of the purchasing manager in a new country location relative to developing suppliers.
7. Develop effective communication between the headquarters' office and the company-world locations.
8. Consider the skills and attitudes necessary to carry out the company purchasing role. Devise development programmes to help to meet local needs.
9. Recognize the many local implications of adherence to rigid specifications *in the planning stage* of a new plant location.
10. Consider the benefits of product grouping by location.

11. Consider setting up a small high-calibre mobile task force to: (a) give aid as necessary to company locations in the operation, organization, or training of local staff or in the development of suppliers, and (b) carry out surveys on new supply markets and plant locations.
12. Where necessary, produce detailed policy and procedure guides to meet local conditions.
13. Encourage liaison between purchasing managers at various locations by exchange visits or regional or international conferences.
14. Consider designs at the conceptual stage against the company-world and not local-market backcloth.

REVERSE MARKETING: THE JAPANESE MODEL

Japanese reverse marketing is a useful conclusion to this chapter. Many of the ideas mentioned earlier have been implemented on a large scale in Japan. Therefore, it is possible to see the longer-term effects of concepts like quality improvement, just-in-time, substantial local reverse marketing, including many small suppliers, continuing improvement, long-term supplier relationships, and extensive single sourcing. Moreover, Japanese companies have perfected reverse marketing at home and abroad.

In order to understand manufacturer–supplier relations in Japan, it must be recognized that industry in Japan is structured in a special way. For example, the large automobile firms Toyota and Nissan are themselves part of larger groups. Also, most large Japanese manufacturers have an "extended company"; for example, Toyota has a large direct interest in many of its direct suppliers, which are not labeled as Toyota "divisions," and exerts indirect control over the firms which in turn supply these firms. These firms may be referred to as the Toyota "family" of companies and a special relationship exists among them.

The unique manufacturer–supplier relationship in Japan results in many firms having a single source for an item, in contrast to the North American multiple sourcing norm. The Japanese also have more specialty and small sources of supply than their North American counterparts. Close, long-term manufacturer–supplier relationships are the rule in Japan with strong loyalties on both sides. Suppliers in Japan are often located close to major manufacturers in order to coordinate their deliveries to the manufacturers' production schedules.

There also seems to be cultural pressure on suppliers to perform well for their manufacturer-customers. Good performance or nonperformance is viewed from a societal perspective. Japanese cultural norms appear to play a large role in the expectations of manufacturer–supplier relationships.

The Hierarchical Structure

In Japan a large manufacturer often forms the top of a pyramid with its primary suppliers or subcontractors forming the first supplier tier (see Figure 6–1). These first-tier suppliers are often controlled by the large manufacturer or, if not controlled, there is a very close relationship between the two firms. An example would be Aisin-Warner which supplies automatic transmissions to Toyota, and is controlled by Toyota which has a 90% ownership. In this case the control is obvious, but there are many cases where direct or indirect control of supplier firms is not as obvious. The first-tier suppliers supply major parts and subassemblies. Aisin-Warner also supplies to other auto assemblers such as Mitsubishi, Isuzu, and Volvo, but does not supply to Toyota's arch-rival, Nissan. These first-tier suppliers have a number of suppliers which form tier 2, which in turn have suppliers supplying components to them forming tier 3. This supplier relationship can extend to five tiers, the last one often consisting of subassembly work done by independent subcontractors in their homes. Generally, the further

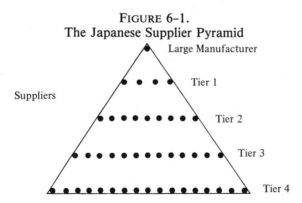

FIGURE 6–1.
The Japanese Supplier Pyramid

down in number of tiers, the more likely will be the use of home workers as suppliers.

Typically, any changes in suppliers are likely to come between lower-level tiers, not between the large manufacturer and tier 1. This is because of the close, long-term relationship between manufacturer and top-tier suppliers. The pyramid relationship is often not as straightforward as presented above. For example, a tier 2 supplier may supply directly to a major manufacturer and also supply to a first-tier supplier.

It is evident that changes in suppliers occur rarely in Japan. New suppliers may be added to the supplier base as new technology and new products provide additional capacity for growth. For an existing supplier to be cut off by the purchaser would be an uncommon event, since purchaser and supplier are expected to work closely together. In return for such stability the purchaser has access to almost all supplier information, can demand high loyalty, influence to whom else the vendor may sell, insist on a nearby location, and exercise extreme pressure to conform to quality, delivery, and quantity expectations.

Supplier Aggressiveness

Suppliers at all tiers appear to be working on very low profit margins. Typically, they share their cost figures with their major manufacturer-customer, with the quoted price for a part or a subassembly very close to their actual costs of production. The incentive for profits puts pressure on the supplier to reduce costs through process efficiency and economies of scale. Workers in supplier firms fully recognize the necessity for cost reduction and efficiency in their employer's ability to survive.

A good example illustrating the seriousness of the focus on cost reduction and cooperation by labor involved a supplier that had just received a major new order from a large manufacturer during the field research for this book in Japan. In order to ensure that the new process was efficient, with costs kept at the absolute minimum, the production employees remained at the plant around the clock during the initial production period. This was not an isolated example—many firms cited similar experiences.

Technical Information Sharing

There is usually close technical cooperation in product development between large manufacturers and first-tier suppliers. This cooperation may take different forms. For example, design engineers from both firms may work as a team on a new product. There may be continued exchange of information, and the supplier firm may be permitted to use the research facilities of the large manufacturer. For example one of the suppliers interviewed used the research facilities of Honda Research and Development Co. Ltd., a wholly owned subsidiary of The Honda Motor Co. Ltd.

Japanese suppliers appear to invest heavily in new product development and in making their production processes more efficient. Manufacturer and supplier will often form a joint task force to address a specific problem. Because of this close liaison, Japanese suppliers seem in a better position to understand and be compatible with the large manufacturers' production processes.

Some Unique Characteristics

In addition to the comments above, additional characteristics of Japanese purchaser–supplier relations include the following:

1. In Japan the control by the purchaser is so extensive it does not seem to require ownership, although ownership does play a part in supplier relations.
2. Staff of large manufacturers quite often move in and out of positions in supplier firms. They may become part of a temporary "project team" or may be moved permanently. It is not unusual to find managers in supplier firms who have come from the major customer/manufacturer.
3. The major manufacturer often has daily contact with its suppliers. The reasons for this may normally extend beyond those simply related to the current order being produced, as would be the standard reason for daily manufacturer-supplier contact in North America. Technical information exchanges and new product information are common reasons for frequent contact.
4. The Japanese manufacturer's willingness and assistance in

ensuring that the supplier is profitable and that suppliers grow is different from the North American norm. Toyota uses the term "mutual prosperity" in reference to its suppliers.

5. The Japanese manufacturer's restrictions regarding other customers to whom the supplier may sell, and what percent of the supplier's production should go to these other customers exhibits a degree of control over the supplier that is rarely seen in North America.

Domestic Supplier Selection

It is unusual for a Japanese purchaser to add or drop suppliers; therefore, the decision to add new suppliers is not exercised very often. A number of purchasers interviewed commented on the tremendous effort their organizations expend in integrating new suppliers into their production process and meeting technical and quality standards. Because of this, the major manufacturers would rather expend additional energy and resources in developing their current suppliers than develop new ones. For example, a manufacturer may insist on having parts or subassemblies delivered in containers compatible with the production machinery, utilize the just-in-time inventory system, and conform to a zero-defects standard of quality. The resulting high cost of introducing and educating new suppliers may account for most major manufacturers having only one supplier for a particular part or subassembly. It is clear that if Japanese manufacturers are so reluctant to add new Japanese suppliers, it would be very difficult for an international supplier to become a supplier to Japan.

Since a supplier who failed to live up to a customer's expectations would have great difficulty securing another customer, the fear of losing a current customer can be seen as a strong deterrent to supplier mismanagement. There are major psychological and economic pressures on Japanese suppliers to perform to their customers' expectations.

The Relationship with MITI

It is no secret that the Ministry of International Trade and Industry (MITI) plays a significant role in most important industrial matters in Japan. MITI uses its all-pervasive influence to induce firms to pursue an approved government strategy by offering tax incentives and low interest loans for specific MITI sanctioned projects. MITI encourages suppliers to adopt the latest technology, such as robotics, with the use of incentives, especially in industries that have been singled out for specific assistance. Thus, either a purchaser or a supplier can approach MITI with a proposition or a project. Similarly MITI may initiate action with purchasers or suppliers.

Subcontractors' Associations

The role of subcontractors' associations is significant in the manufacturer–supplier relationship. For example, the All-Japan Subcontractors' Promotion Association, which is affiliated with MITI, is the coordinating body of 47 associations at the prefecture* level. The prefecture level associations facilitate the distribution of contracts from large manufacturers to its many subcontractor members. The association also acts as a conduit of information between the manufacturer and its subcontractor suppliers and as a buffer in the settlement of disputes.

Supplier associations composed of suppliers of one large manufacturer are also formed, often upon the initiative of the manufacturer. For example, there are three supplier associations consisting of firms that supply principally to Toyota. These associations work hand-in-hand with the major manufacturer on specific problems, such as improved quality levels, specific new technology, or improved production processes.

Reverse Marketing in and outside of Japan

The aggressive seeking out of new domestic sources of supply by manufacturers is almost nonexistent in Japan. Typically, manufacturers are approached by current and potential suppliers with new product proposals and new technology ideas. The addition of new suppliers is an infrequent occurrence, and if it does occur, it is usually based on new technology which neither the manufac-

---

*In Japan prefects are provinces similar to states in the United States.

turer nor its current suppliers possess. Rarely do large manufacturers have to seek out new sources of supply. Thus, the initiative lies with the suppliers, not the purchasers.

Internationally, new reverse marketing is more common, as Japanese purchasers aggressively pursue sources of raw materials or suppliers in low-wage countries to fulfill specific needs that cannot be met domestically. Two examples given were that of a steel company which is continually seeking new sources of iron ore world-wide, and a watch company that is trying to ensure that assembly and subassembly operations can be carried out in low-wage countries.

New concepts are challenging supply managers all over the world. The inevitable conclusion is that continuing improvement is the only long-term realistic goal. Specific tools and concepts that appear exciting today may lose their appeal. The challenge of continuing improvement, however, will remain. And as long as the goal of improvement remains, reverse marketing in one form or another with existing or new suppliers will also be required.

BRIEF SUMMARY

1. Major trends in the field of materials management congruent with reverse marketing include a greater emphasis on quality, MRP and JIT, learning curve, computerization and advanced communications technology, longer-term contracts, single sourcing, and continuing improvement.

2. Global companies view the world as their market and supply base and use reverse marketing to provide a strategic edge.

3. The Japanese use reverse marketing constantly to help improve the performance of long-term continuing suppliers domestically. Outside of Japan, Japanese purchasers use reverse marketing to acquire a competitive edge on resources and raw materials, a new technology, access to a low-cost labor pool, or to meet local content requirements.

4. In Japan suppliers share cost information with purchasers and there is also a close technological exchange with people, and facilities.

CHAPTER 7

Reverse Marketing and Supplier Size

SUPPLIER size may be an important factor in any reverse marketing effort. Obviously, certain requirements are more appropriately met by small suppliers, others by large sources. The size of the supplier will affect the way the development should be planned and implemented. Although considerable purchaser aggressiveness may be called for regardless of supply size, the successful approach to a small supplier may not work with a larger vendor.

In this chapter several examples will be used to highlight the key differences between developing small and large suppliers. The small supplier situation will be looked at first.

REVERSE MARKETING AND SMALL SUPPLIERS

If any case has to be made for the need for reverse marketing, the small supplier fits admirably. The small supplier is identified here as any organization in which one person (often the owner/ manager) makes all of the key decisions. Almost by definition, a small supplier tends to be vulnerable. In the first place, it is dependent on one key person's personal strengths and weaknesses. A small supplier will also be limited in resources, and may lack financial strength, R&D resources, or depth in typical functional areas such as marketing, accounting, or production. Conventional procurement wisdom states that purchasers should only deal with vendors who do not exhibit such weaknesses. What then is the case for developing small suppliers? The first argument is an easy one. If the purchaser does not take the initiative, the small supplier, because of a lack of marketing aggressiveness, may never appear. This still does not answer why the purchaser should even bother with developing small sources. And the answers to this latter question will be apparent after some examples have been given.

CASE: NICOR

NICOR was a large manufacturer of abrasives, tapes, and copying machines. Although the abrasives and tapes were produced in the company's factory, the copying machines had originally been assembled from parts primarily sourced offshore. However, there was top management pressure to source copying machine components domestically. Cal Stiller, NICOR's Director of Purchases, therefore tried to develop as many national sources of supply as possible.

Dan Meredith had been a local distributor of electrical parts who had subsequently given up the distributorship and commenced manufacturing parts. During Cal Stiller's first effort at developing local suppliers, he approached Dan Meredith to see if he would be interested in doing special windings for a pilot project. At that time, Meredith was engaged in subcontract work for a few companies and also did some work for the government. He owned his own building and employed eight people. Meredith was not too interested in the windings, but Stiller insisted that he should try them just the same. Because of Stiller's insistence Meredith decided to take on the windings, an order of $4500. He delivered them on time and they were of good quality.

Two years later, Meredith came to Stiller and said: "I really need some business, I'll do anything, wind, assemble, or whatever you need done—I'll give it a try." At this time the production lines at NICOR were overcrowded and Stiller asked Meredith to assemble back panels and make some resistor assemblies. Meredith continued to be a good supplier. He delivered on time and was consistently in the preferred range of the quality limits established by NICOR's engineers. From then on, NICOR used Meredith almost as a plant overload service. His close proximity was an important factor in this role. Stiller could telephone him and within half an hour, Meredith would be at the plant with a truck to pick up work, deliver a few parts needed in a hurry, or to discuss a problem that had just cropped up. Many times Stiller helped Meredith by buying materials or parts for him or by sending an engineer over to give him advice.

Five years after the original Meredith order for the windings, NICOR needed a supplier for BQX circuits used in copying machines. The circuits had been imported at a rate of 40,000 per year at a laid down cost of $3.75 each. After six months of trying to locate a suitable national supplier, the best price Stiller could get was $4.05 per unit. A discussion of this problem with the NICOR plant manager revealed that NICOR had some equipment that could be used to produce the circuit boards but the employees who ran the machines were reluctant to work on other tasks when there was no circuit board work for them. A further consideration was the need for more space in the plant. In a discussion with plant engineers, the plant manager had indicated that if any part of the operation was to be moved outside, the circuit board assembly would be the first to go.

Stiller called Dan Meredith to see whether he would be interested in manufacturing the required circuit boards. Meredith expressed interest but saw all kinds of problems. "I have no machinery, no labor, and no real skills," he said. "We might be able to help you there," replied Stiller. The result: all of NICOR's circuit board assembly equipment was transferred to Meredith's plant. The equipment had been fully depreciated but was in good working order. NICOR engineers helped Meredith get started. He hired and trained his own operators and was able to deliver circuit boards to NICOR at $3.00 each.

Twelve months after manufacture of circuit boards started, Meredith received his first order for circuit boards from a company other than NICOR. Subsequently, Meredith bought modern new equipment because his current circuit board production had outgrown the capacity and quality of his earlier machines. He also installed air conditioning equipment in his plant for "clean room" facilities. Twelve years after his first NICOR order, Meredith employed 70 people and had excellent employee relations. His total business with NICOR amounted to about one-third of his total sales. Twice Dan Meredith was featured in NICOR's quarterly employee news magazine, and once in NICOR's annual report.

Reverse Marketing Insights from NICOR

The NICOR case illustrates that a small local supplier can develop into a viable long-term source, although it can take a long time. Had Dan Meredith refused to take the initial order for windings, the one he did not really need, he might not have received the second order, the one he really did need. Stiller's foresight in developing him as a supplier before a pressing need arose helped both purchaser and supplier in this instance.

Useful to both parties was the proximity of the small supplier to the purchaser. This allowed for frequent consultation between the principals involved and for quick action on any problem. It also facilitated special assistance by engineering and purchasing. Both parties took advantage of their proximity to each other and turned it to their mutual benefit. Stiller was dealing directly with the owner/manager of the supplying firm and this certainly enhanced the speed in which major decisions could be made.

BENEFITS.   The major benefits arising out of this small reverse marketing can be easily identified. First, the purchaser received the following benefits:

1. Special windings when it was difficult to find a suitable source for a relatively small order.
2. Local content for items formally imported. Presumably, this facilitated sales to public customers who required minimum local content. It also met a corporate objective.
3. Local printed circuit boards at $3.00 versus $3.75. This not only resulted in an annual price saving of $30,000, but also freed up inventory, capacity, and labor in NICOR's plant and made the plant manager happy.
4. An emergency standby source for quick delivery of small requirements. This may have resulted in price savings, but probably far more significantly, it helped insure on-time delivery of finished products to NICOR customers and avoided stock-out and schedule interruption costs.
5. Favorable publicity for the purchasing department in employee magazines and the annual report. Successful small reverse marketing makes good news. The procurement function, not usually favored by an internal and external press, can significantly benefit from such exposure.

The vendor, Dan Meredith, received the following benefits:

1. Business when he needed volume to keep going.
2. Assistance in a variety of ways:

   a. Materials supplied by the purchaser to avoid capital tie ups, possibly delays, higher prices, and additional quality and inspection resources.
   b. Technical advice, personal visits from engineering or technical staff to assist in training or overcoming specific technical problems when required.
   c. Equipment to manufacture printed circuit boards. Facilitated entry into a new business at low cost and at little risk.
   d. A gradual increase in orders to control growth.

   This assistance might have been expensive for Meredith had he been required to purchase it at regular market rates.

3. An opportunity to get into new markets and new products with a base volume assured by NICOR.
4. Additional business from other customers because of skills, equipment, and opportunities originated with NICOR.
5. An opportunity to grow over the years without overextending himself in the process and a building of strengths and size simultaneously.
6. A quality reputation in the trade. The exacting standards and quality assurance programs of NICOR made it possible for Dan Meredith to establish a quality reputation.
7. A highly flexible manufacturing organization with quick turnaround capability. Over the years, Dan Meredith developed a reputation not only for quality, but also for responsiveness and quick delivery time, a valuable competitive asset.
8. A sound, stable, core customer with a good reputation whose business provided an opportunity to grow financially and technologically.

It is easy to see the attractions that reverse marketing holds for small companies, both purchaser and vendor. Both sides can benefit substantially, and even in unsuspected ways if the relationship is managed well over time.

It is possible to oversell the benefits of reverse marketing with small suppliers without identifying the pitfalls, however. One simple example, where the purchaser gave the development a serious try, follows.

CASE: NEWMAN COMPANY

Mary Decarie, Director of Purchases for Hudson Corporation, fully intended to develop as many local sources of supply as possible for the items needed for the firm's new generation of elevating equipment. Jack Newman, owner and manager of Newman Company, had started a machine shop about fifteen years earlier using surplus equipment. His company had grown from three employees to 25 since then. Decarie went to see Newman to discuss the machining of two relatively simple castings which Hudson currently purchased from a distant supplier. She wanted a local supplier not only to reduce freight costs but also to be able to have more frequent and closer communication with a firm nearby.

Decarie cautioned Newman that although the specifications on these parts were not too difficult to meet, the handling requirements were different from the ones that Newman had used on routine orders in his shop. A trial order was agreed upon for 200 pieces, with the provision that a Hudson inspector would inspect the first 25 pieces completed. The inspector rejected the entire lot. When Newman complained about the outright rejection, Decarie explained that the dimensional control on the parts was not at fault but that the parts' appearance was not acceptable—they were full of stains, fingerprints, tool marks, nicks, and scratches. Decarie suggested that a Hudson engineer visit Newman's plant to give assistance before any more pieces were produced. Newman complained about the delay and the tie-up of his machinery so Decarie made arrangements with the chief engineer to send a person to the Newman company immediately.

The engineer stayed two full days at Newman's plant and oversaw the machining of two 25-piece lots which also had to be rejected. The engineer concluded that the only way anyone could illustrate to Newman how the parts could be machined satisfactorily was to show him the process. Newman had been very insistent that Hudson Corporation was either wrong in its specifications or else shooting for the moon, and had questioned every suggestion made by the engineer.

Decarie then contacted Hudson's regular supplier for the parts and asked if she could bring Newman on a tour of their facilities to examine how they were able to produce the part successfully. The supplier agreed and Hudson Corporation paid Newman's expenses to visit the supplier.

Upon his return Newman exclaimed about the operation to which he had been exposed. "It was more like a hospital than a machine shop," Newman said. "Everyone in that shop was wearing a mask, special coat, gloves, and covers over their shoes. They put some kind of chemical or oil on each part right after each operation. I have never seen anything like it before."

Decarie asked Newman if he was now ready to machine the parts to the specifications and Newman assured Decarie that he was. Several days passed before Decarie received another rejection report from the quality control group. Newman Company was still not able to produce even one piece to specifications. The next day Decarie visited the Newman plant and found that the employees still were not wearing protective clothing or gloves and that the inhibiter they were trying to use was the incorrect type for the particular alloy of the castings. Decarie then told Newman to forget about the whole contract, whereupon Newman protested that his shop had already completed 100 parts and that his machinery had been tied up on this small order for a long time. Decarie replied that Newman had forgotten about the cost of ruined castings to Hudson, not to mention the time spent by Hudson's engineers, inspectors, and herself, and all the trouble and expense of sending Newman to visit the current casting supplier.

This example not only shows that reverse marketing success is not automatically guaranteed; it also identifies the problem of when to abort a development effort. How long should the purchaser persist before giving up? Unless the small supplier shows at least a minimum amount of interest in making the deal a success, it is clearly impossible for the purchaser to drag the supplier along all the way. It was most unusual for Mary Decarie to request an existing vendor to show its operations to a potential competitor. Clearly, Jack Newman did not appreciate the lengths to which she went to assist him, and failed to live up to expectations. It is easy to say, in retrospect, that Mary Decarie may have started with the wrong individual in this case. It is possible that with another small vendor and the same assistance she would have had better luck.

Supplier Assistance

The Newman example raises the question as to how far the purchaser should go in extending assistance to a small supplier. There seems to be a need for balance between as little as possible, on the one hand, and just as much as is required to result in successful reverse marketing, on the other. With small suppliers, there may be a need to give far more assistance than would be required in the case of larger suppliers. The small supplier must also want the development to be a success and be willing to work towards that end. Otherwise, it would be simpler for the purchaser to make the items or parts under consideration in its own plant or buy them elsewhere.

There is an increasing trend toward employees of larger firms leaving the firm to start a business of their own. These entrepreneurs usually experience growing pains with start-up and often are amenable to financial and technical assistance. The payoff in the purchasing firm's assistance is often a reliable supply source from someone who understands the corporate culture of the buyer, an important aspect that can take years to build with a totally new supplier.

The need for supplier assistance tends to be greatest with small suppliers. Apart from the need to extend such assistance to assure success, other considerations may be involved. For example, a common problem for many small suppliers is a shortage of cash or working capital. This may be a significant obstacle to a successful development effort. Recognizing the problem, a purchaser may employ a number of remedies. Some of these were used in the two small reverse marketing examples already cited. A quick listing could include: supplying materials or parts, purchaser ownership of tools, dies, and fixtures, lending equipment, providing technical or other assistance, advance payments, progress payments, payments upon delivery, assistance in obtaining loans from financial institutions, or direct loans. No matter which form this assistance actually takes, it is important to recognize four facts:

1. The assistance may be critical in assuring development success.
2. There is an actual cost to the purchaser to provide this assistance.
3. If the small supplier had to purchase this assistance in the

open market it would probably be expensive in terms of both time and money.

4. The purchaser's actual cost of providing the assistance may be substantially lower than the vendor's perceived cost for acquiring the same in the open market.

These four facts add up to the following conclusions:

1. The amount and form of assistance needs to be structured as part of the whole deal.

2. Since the assistance may be low cost to the purchaser and of high value to the vendor, it represents a golden opportunity to use it as a lever to secure something else in return. In other words, there is no need for purchasers to set up a form of charity agency to help ailing small suppliers to survive. To the contrary, the aid should be dispensed as part of a sound business deal. And in return, the purchaser should get back the equivalent value. This may be in the form of lower price, such as NICOR received in the Dan Meredith case. It may also be unusually fast delivery, willingness to respond instantaneously to emergencies, willing acceptance of additional orders without quoting ridiculous lead times or prices, unusually stringent quality standards, or anything else that will be of high value to the purchaser. This opportunity for barter using relatively low cost assistance that is nevertheless of high value to the vendor is probably unique to small vendors. As vendors grow, the need for such assistance declines.

There are, of course, always situations where assistance to the small supplier may not be necessary at all, or may be minimal at best. The Kemp situation is an excellent example of a case where purchasing initiative was necessary to get the ball rolling, but where the supplier quickly took over the helm.

CASE: KEMP CORPORATION

Kemp Corporation was a small progressive firm founded in Canada by two engineers. The two founders set a company goal of supplying high-quality, low-volume, intricate tooling and machining work on special alloys for a reasonable price. Mary Decarie, director of purchases at Hudson Corporation, first heard of this company when she attended a conference about manufacturing problems in space-age technology in Chicago.

When Hudson was gearing up for production of its new generation of computerized, low-energy hoisting equipment, she was unable to find a suitable source for the main selector shaft, the most important part of the unit and one that required great machining skills. After a fruitless search among U.S. suppliers, Decarie sent Kemp Corporation a set of blueprints and specifications and requested a quotation. Kemp Corporation submitted a surprisingly low quotation with a good delivery date. After further investigation, Decarie awarded it the machining contract for the selector shaft. The order was received, found to be of exceptionally good quality and subsequently Kemp was given other machinery business by Decarie.

A year later, Decarie was considering enlarging Kemp Corporation's orders by asking it to machine several other parts in addition to the selector shafts. She was concerned about the high volume of component parts Hudson was importing and wondered if she might persuade Kemp Corporation to establish a U.S. subsidiary. She proposed this idea to Kemp's vice president of sales who called on Decarie once every three months. The vice president of sales, who expressed immediate interest in the idea, said he would discuss it with the firm's two founders. Three months later, Decarie was informed that Kemp Corporation's founders had, in principle, approved expansion into the United States. They wanted to visit the United States to select manufacturing space and to discuss government regulations. Decarie suggested that they prepare a list of tooling and equipment they would intend to move to the United States. She also promised to take the two founders to the state capitol to help them in their discussions with government officials. Shortly afterward, the two founders visited the United States and quickly found suitable manufacturing space. Decarie then took them to meet with representatives of the state's industrial development office. Decarie had written the government in advance and in one day the founders were able to make all the necessary arrangements.

Kemp moved its equipment to the new U.S. operation and began training local labor. The U.S. Kemp Corporation, right from the start, did machining work of quality which compared favorably with that of the Canadian parent. Subsequently, Decarie placed an increasing amount of business with the firm and was very pleased with the results.

Decarie said about the Kemp Corporation:

> We found them to be a good supplier from the start. When I
> first talked to them about moving to the United States, I was
> quite willing to give them a five-year contract or some assurance
> of business of that kind. It turned out that the Kemp founders
> did not ask for any assurance of business as they were so sure
> that they would have no trouble finding sales in the United
> States. I felt somewhat responsible since I had talked them into
> coming to the United States in the first place.

The real savings to Hudson came in lower freight costs and
elimination of import duties, a total saving of about 15%. In addition, they were buying U.S. made parts from a supplier which was
close to their own plant.

A specialist in its own right, Kemp Corporation reacted quickly
to Hudson's reverse marketing efforts with the decision to establish a U.S. subsidiary. Kemp's small size limited its ability to seek
out customers initially. Its strengths in manufacturing know-how
offset this marketing weakness with the result that the development efforts required by Hudson were only minimal. Indicative
of the relationship established between the supplier and the purchaser in this case was Kemp's responsiveness to the idea of establishing a U.S. subsidiary. Decarie's insight into Kemp's needs was
shown by her offer of assistance to Kemp in the one area that
really needed help, its dealings with local government. In this case
the purchaser would have been willing to offer far more assistance
than the supplier wanted. Decarie was ready to stand by to ensure
sufficient business (a five-year contract) so that the U.S. subsidiary could reach an economic operating level. She would also have
been willing to assist in the selection of a plant site and the hiring
of new labor. It was to Kemp's credit that it was able to manage
on its own.

Small Supplier Dependence

A significant danger, of course, with small suppliers is their dependence on the purchaser. If a single purchaser takes a large percentage of the small supplier's total business or capacity, the small
supplier could be vulnerable if all or a significant amount of business were to be suddenly withdrawn. Some purchasers may favor

such dependence on the argument it gives them greater clout with the vendor. Others may wish to minimize the risk by setting an upper limit on the total amount of business they are willing to place with the small supplier. For example, NICOR tried very hard to keep their business with Dan Meredith below the 33 percent mark and actively encouraged Dan Meredith to seek other customers as a condition of obtaining more sales to NICOR. Since most small suppliers tend to be local, the unfavorable publicity surrounding the bankruptcy of a small local vendor may be a high cost to the purchaser.

Dependence on the purchaser may take a different form, however. If the purchaser continues to provide the same form of assistance over time, one danger may well be that the vendor will take it for granted and fail to improve significant shortcomings. For example, continuing to provide an inspection service may not encourage the vendor to develop internal quality control strength. Continuing to find customers for the small vendor may further weaken marketing initiative and skills.

On the assumption that it is in the best interest of both purchaser and the small supplier that the supplier learns to do without assistance over time, some targets need to be set by both sides to work towards that end. In the case of Kemp Corporation, obviously, Kemp did not ask for and did not expect any assistance and preferred to go it alone. In the case of Dan Meredith, he received a substantial amount of assistance over a long period of time.

It is useful to make a distinction between a purchaser's assistance to a supplier and a close working relationship with good communication. It is possible, especially with a small local vendor, whose manager is in regular contact with purchasing and other company personnel, to develop an excellent working relationship with great communication between the various parties. Ideally, this should exist with all vendors and is not unique to reverse marketing. Supplier assistance goes well beyond the limits of such normal working relationships.

Direct Contact

One of the advantages of dealing with small local vendors is the opportunity to talk directly with the vendor's owner/manager. He or she is likely to give a quick answer, communication is face to face, and a deal is struck quickly, or denied quickly. It does not take particularly long to assess the small supplier's capability and weak and strong points. Moreover, since the size of the deal to the purchaser is not likely to be large, a relatively informal arrangement is probably appropriate for both parties. Actually, this makes reverse marketing for small firms a lot of fun. It is a form of frontier purchasing which allows the purchaser to swagger a bit. It is also a good opportunity to practice reverse marketing skills. The buyer or purchaser can handle the deal personally, visit the supplier's premises, talk to the vendor's current customers locally, and wheel and deal and negotiate on such issues as assistance and benefits to be achieved by both parties. Since small vendors are best suited for small requirements, the question of price may well be secondary to other procurement objectives such as quality, quick delivery, availability, flexibility, and service. Small suppliers may be more loyal than large ones and success may be fairly easily achieved. If successful, the reverse marketing experience with small firms may make excellent news with a high public relations impact inside and outside the purchaser's organization.

Reverse Marketing with Small Firms and Public Relations

A positive local reverse marketing effort with small firms facilitates top management's efforts at community relations. Often top managers are approached locally at the Chamber of Commerce, at local golf, racquet, and service clubs, or at board meetings for local charities by owners/managers of small local businesses. Their question "Why are you not buying anything from me?" deserves to be answered in a more positive manner than "Well, I'll just have to look into that." If the executive can answer: "We have a program aimed at increasing local content and you may know that companies X, Y, and Z have already benefited from it. Anybody locally seriously interested in latching onto this should contact Bill Allison or Heather Carrothers in purchasing," then the executive will find local life much more pleasant. This is a consideration purchasing may not have been sufficiently sensitive to in the past. The same arguments, of course, hold with minority sources, most of which tend to be small suppliers. Many of the difficulties encountered by purchasers with minority sources are typical small reverse marketing problems. Overcoming these successfully enhances the public image of the purchaser's organization.

Successful reverse marketing efforts with small suppliers, like Dan Meredith's case, make excellent internal and external news. These situations can be written up in employee magazines, in annual reports, and in the local press. It may well be that one of the greatest values of small reverse marketing may be its public relations impact. Purchasing concern over helping the organization look good to the local community cannot help but improve purchasing's own image at the same time.

Some reverse marketing initiatives, which may seem small and insignificant to the purchaser with respect to effort expended, may be quite significant to the supplier and might well be a pivotal point in its development as a company. Several examples follow.

A vendor with a good product but with seasonal production scheduling and sales resulting in cash flow problems was assisted when the buyer's purchasing organization agreed to take delivery at a regular flow throughout the year. Rescheduled dating assisted the supplier's cash flow considerably.

A municipality, experiencing difficulty in convincing large traffic-sign producers to supply its specific needs in small quantities, developed a small, local sheet metal stamping company to supply its needs by using the municipality's contacts with other potential users to develop a viable market for the vendor.

A similar situation saw a large multinational tobacco company work hand in hand with a small plastics company to produce a new tobacco container designed by the firm's R&D people. Assistance included financial and technical aid and an exclusive six-year contract. The payoff for the tobacco company was a very popular new line and the supplier built up a business using the same technology (but not the identical packaging) for other customers.

In another instance, the corrugated carton industry in one geographical area was controlled by five major suppliers. A large user of corrugated cartons discovered a small nonunion supplier located in a small town, which wanted to break into the market. Reverse marketing started with several orders with assistance at each step, culminating in lower prices, faster delivery, and with the small firm eventually becoming a major player in the industry competing head to head with the big five.

The common thread in the above examples is that the effort expended by the purchaser loomed large in importance to the developed supplier. A single reverse marketing initiative can be the take-off point for the developed firm.

REVERSE MARKETING AND LARGE SUPPLIERS

The development of large suppliers is attractive for one major reason: the potential payoffs. That's where the money is. It may be fun and good publicity to develop small suppliers, but the purchaser interested in the really big savings and the really big deals is going to have to develop large suppliers. And the fun will not be there in the same way it was with small suppliers. Large suppliers are notoriously bureaucratic, difficult to deal with, slow to respond, and may be reluctant to jump enthusiastically at new deals. Large reverse marketing may require unusual purchaser perseverance, preparation, imagination, and aggressiveness within the purchaser's own organization as well as with the vendor's personnel. Almost invariably, large reverse marketing will end up being a team or task force effort with a time horizon from months to years. A high degree of formality may characterize the proceedings. Top management will probably have to be fully involved. Feasibility studies will have to be prepared by the purchaser to prove the viability of the proposal.

Examples in earlier chapters have showed some of the real advantages of the large supplier. In the Panelectronics situation, Vencor, the large supplier, possessed the R&D and financial strength necessary to undertake the development of a new alloy, whereas the smaller vendor could not cope. In the Mega Technologies case, the large vendors had the marketing strength to take full advantage of the R&D investment required up front. When General Motors needed platinum for its catalytic converter it turned to reverse marketing and the creation of a new mine to satisfy its substantial requirements.

The following example illustrates a small firm's experience in convincing a large supplier to supply. A small steel user saw many advantages in having a large multinational U.S. owned steel producer as a supplier, such as expertise in steel of all types, price, availability, and U.S. content. The problem was to convince the large steel producer to supply directly. An education job was necessary and executives from the steel producer were invited to the purchaser's plant to explain who they were and to show that they were serious. The purchaser talked about the firm's total steel requirements, rather than breaking it down by division, to give a bigger impact. The education effort paid off when the large steel firm agreed not only to supply steel but to open up its other services such as steel research and development data to the purchaser.

One of the most interesting cases involving large reverse marketing and one illustrating the key difference between small and large reverse marketing is that of Clair Chemical Corporation.

CASE: CLAIR CHEMICAL CORPORATION

Clair Chemical Corporation (CCC), a large multinational chemical company with headquarters in New York, had a substantial corporate procurement group under the leadership of vice president John Beck. Beck had a reputation as an aggressive and imaginative deal maker and he traveled around the world at least once a year to look for opportunities. Several years earlier he had been the sparkplug behind a particularly attractive long-term natural gas contract for CCC's northeastern main production complex. By using a coal back-up system CCC was able to buy interruptable natural gas at very low prices. This contract permitted CCC to compete aggressively on a substantial range of petrochemical products. The contract also allowed for substantial future growth. Since Beck was so heavily involved in major reverse marketing efforts, his director of purchases was fully in charge of day-to-day operations in corporate procurement.

One day, upon returning from a month-long overseas trip, John Beck heard that Bernier, a large Swiss chemical firm, was planning to build an anhydrous ammonia and fertilizer plant near Boston and had already purchased the site. Beck was interested in this news because CCC purchased about $40 million worth of anhydrous ammonia from a New Jersey plant. He discussed the plant proposal with Bernier representatives in Boston and found that actual construction of the plant was scheduled to start in about nine months. He also found out that Bernier intended to manufacture anhydrous ammonia from residual oil which they intended to import from Venezuela. The first step of this process was to obtain hydrogen gas from the oil, a complex process resulting in the creation of some environmentally undesirable by-products. Beck immediately thought that Bernier should be interested in using natural gas rather than oil to produce hydrogen. The extraction of hydrogen from natural gas was a process less complex than that using petroleum and resulted in a pure product with fewer undesirable by-products. The second step in Beck's thinking was that, since he had access to attractively priced natural gas at CCC's main northeastern production complex, perhaps Bernier might be interested in obtaining this natural gas for itself. In that way Bernier could sell anhydrous ammonia and hydrogen to CCC at highly favorable prices.

Gaining Internal Support

John Beck discussed his ideas with Stan Olson, executive vice president at CCC. Olson agreed that the logic was sound but had doubts about actually going ahead with the talks.

> OLSON: I am afraid you're fishing behind this net, John. Bernier has already committed itself too far now to turn back. If we ourselves were in Bernier's shoes, we would never pull back a capital project as far advanced as this. Just look at it. They already have all of their plans ready. They have even purchased the plant site. I'm afraid you'll be wasting our time and theirs on this one.

> BECK: Stan, what do we have to lose? This could be a great deal for us and for them. Let me at least have a quick look at the full economics of it so that we can realistically assess what we are talking about. All I need now is a small team to do some quick and dirty technical and feasibility work to tell us what the ballpark figures look like. We have some sharp people in our development group and I'm sure they can give us a handle on this thing within a few weeks.

> OLSON: I'm willing to ask Harry Johnston [vice president for development] if he is willing to take this on, but I want him to know I am highly skeptical. Let me see if he is in right now.

Harry Johnston agreed with Olson that the idea was a long shot at best and that it sounded like a wild goose chase. However, Beck presented his plans in a manner that made them worth pursuing.

> JOHNSTON: We have lots of sound projects on the go right now and I'd hate to pull some people out for a wild one like this.

> BECK: Harry, you and I have worked on a lot of deals together. Some worked out, some did not. I cannot guarantee you that we

will be successful on this one. However, I can tell you right now that I suspect there is a lot of money to be made here if we can get something going. But to confirm that suspicion I am going to need a few of your good people for a little while. If I am wrong, I owe you a bottle of the finest wine you care to specify. [Harry had a reputation as a wine connoisseur.] But, if I am right, I would like you to agree right now to give me more help in the future, because we are going to have to move fast and you have the technical and economics experts required to push it through the next stages.

JOHNSTON: John, I'll take you up on that deal, because I'm looking forward to taking a bottle off you and because I don't think I'm risking very much.

BECK (addressing both executives): Because time is of the essence here, do I have the agreement from both of you to help me push this through the next few weeks? As soon as we have the information, I would like to sit down with both of you to decide whether we proceed or drop the whole idea.

Stan Olson and Harry Johnston agreed to give it a push, and within ten days the development group had completed a preliminary feasibility study. Olson, Johnston, and Beck discussed the findings. The thirty-page study showed that it would require an investment of about $50 million to build an economical plant near CCC's site to manufacture hydrogen and anhydrous ammonia. A major portion of the anhydrous ammonia produced could be used by CCC, but the remainder would have to be sold as fertilizer. The study also showed that annual savings for CCC could exceed $10 million on anhydrous ammonia alone. Moreover, CCC was also a large producer of hydrogen gas. It produced its own hydrogen through the electrolysis of water, an expensive process. Should Bernier build near the CCC site, CCC would be able to buy hydrogen as well as anhydrous ammonia. Beck said: "Even though we make hydrogen ourselves now, that doesn't mean we shouldn't consider buying it cheaper elsewhere." Potential savings on hydrogen might even exceed those on the ammonia.

John Beck asked Stan Olson whether CCC might actually erect such a plant should the Bernier deal fall through. Olson replied: "It might be done, but I'm not too anxious to get started in the fertilizer business. I also doubt if any other executive at CCC knows much about the fertilizer business and would care to get into it." Harry Johnston wholeheartedly agreed with Stan Olson.

The three men agreed that the project showed enough promise to warrant further exploration with Bernier. Nevertheless, both Stan Olson and Harry Johnston remained skeptical about Bernier's response. In this, they were certainly correct.

Preliminary negotiations with Bernier representatives showed that Bernier was only lukewarm about John Beck's proposal. Beck found out that the plant Bernier intended to build near Boston was an exact replica of a similar plant just completed in Italy. The use of natural gas would require the design of a completely different plant. Moreover, as Bernier executives quickly pointed out, Bernier had already purchased the plant site and was too far committed at this point of time.

Beck told them that he could see real advantages to Bernier in their move to CCC's production complex. First, they would have a guaranteed outlet for a significant part of their total sales volume. Second, they would be offered natural gas at terms they would be unable to match anywhere else. Third, the extraction of hydrogen from natural gas was a simpler, cleaner process, which resulted in a purer product. The Bernier representatives told Beck that any change of plans would have to be approved by the head office in Geneva, Switzerland, but that they were sufficiently impressed with Beck's proposal to bring it to the attention of the head-office executives.

Checking Other Potential Suppliers

Once John Beck had started talking to Bernier representatives and after he had read the report of the CCC development group, he decided that he might as well try to see if he could interest other fertilizer producers in the same idea. Should Bernier decide against the proposal, or should another firm offer better terms, CCC would still benefit from the same basic idea. Beck first found out which companies were reported interested in building an ammonia plant. Then he made an appointment with the president or the vice president of sales for each company to discuss the possibility of building their plant at the CCC site. Beck talked to four interested parties. One dropped out almost immediately because it lacked sufficient money. Two others declined because their plans were a little closer to completion. The fourth made a study of its own and indicated a strong interest.

In the meantime, John Beck kept pressing local Bernier representatives, who insisted that they had taken it as far as they could and that Switzerland really controlled the purse strings. When, after four months, he still had not heard any word from Bernier in Switzerland, Beck made appointments for Olson, Johnston, and himself with the Swiss executives and flew over.

The Swiss Visit

The Swiss executives were at first suspicious of the three CCC representatives. They had not really prepared themselves for this visit and wondered if someone was trying to pull the wool over their eyes. It soon became evident to them, however, that the CCC men knew exactly what they were talking about. Impressed by the CCC representatives, the Bernier executives soon discarded their suspicions. A strong attraction in CCC's offer was the guaranteed combined purchase of hydrogen and anhydrous ammonia. What made CCC's offer even more attractive was that it had an even demand throughout the year, preventing any need for inventory and guaranteeing a reasonable operating level of the plant year round.

The Swiss executives of Bernier were unable to promise the CCC team anything definite. They did say that they were very much interested, but that they still had to study the details for themselves. They were concerned about the location of CCC's plant site in relation to their market. They also wanted to determine freight factors and the availability of other raw materials. They were also concerned about the eventual disposition of the plant site near Boston and the acquisition of a new site near CCC. They did promise to delay the scheduled beginning of construction on the Boston site until they had decided on CCC's offer.

During the next four months Bernier personnel made a thorough study of CCC's proposal. Many transatlantic phone calls were made and a team of Bernier executives and technical experts came to visit the CCC site. Almost ten months after the initial contact, Bernier was ready to sit down for final negotiations.

The Negotiations

Four Bernier executives flew to New York to take part in the final negotiations with CCC. These representatives were the president, the vice president in charge of overseas affairs, the manager of

American operations, and the solicitor. Representing CCC was a negotiation team of three people. John Beck was in charge, aided by CCC's general counsel and Harry Johnston. Several other CCC executives or specialists were called in from time to time for advice. The negotiations lasted about two and a half weeks and a ten-year contract was signed. Bernier would build a new plant and would buy its gas at CCC's cost. Special arrangements were made to make interruptable gas firm through the same plan that CCC intended to use in its own plant. CCC guaranteed a base price for both hydrogen and anhydrous ammonia and an even annual demand rate.

Negotiations with the other fertilizer producer had preceded the Bernier negotiations. John Beck was not anxious to conclude this second negotiation prior to a full exploration of the Bernier deal. He had, therefore, put the other negotiations on hold pending the outcome of the Bernier proposal. Before final agreement with Bernier was reached, CCC's negotiation team adjourned the negotiation for several days. During this time further negotiations with the other party showed that the Bernier deal was more favorable. Consequently, final agreement was reached with Bernier and construction started about six months later.

John Beck commented that it had been a very tough year for everyone involved at CCC. Several times hopes had been high that agreement might be possible, only to be dashed again shortly thereafter. He also concluded:

> So many of our top executives and technical people got involved in this project in one form or another during these past twelve months. In the end, I had the feeling that if we had been unsuccessful with both Bernier and the other company, we would have gone ahead and built the plant ourselves, anyway. We had been so busy convincing outsiders what a good deal it was for them, that it was difficult to see why it wouldn't be a good deal if we decided to go it alone.

The Bernier Deal and Reverse Marketing Implications

The CCC example contains most of the elements of a typical large reverse marketing effort. The need for top management involvement, the need to commit significant resources from a variety of disciplines to prepare a feasibility study, the need to overcome internal resistance and skepticism, the need to overcome supplier reluctance, and the need for perseverance are all evident in this outstanding example. It is ironic that, in the end, the possibility of make-or-buy, firmly ruled out by CCC's top executives at the start, regained stature. It is probably inevitable that make-or-buy should be a serious consideration in large reverse marketing projects. The purchaser is forced to do the homework and to prepare a formal proposal that makes it attractive to the large supplier. It is only logical that under the circumstances the question of going it alone needs to be looked at seriously.

The formal proposal has a second benefit. The purchaser cannot afford to let control over the development effort slip into the vendor's hands. By committing a proposal to paper, the purchaser increases the chance that this proposal will be passed to the appropriate decision makers and in the form the purchaser wants it to be. Since it may not always be clear in a large company where the key decision maker is, the problem of assuring that the proposal gets serious consideration by the supplier is not to be minimized. In the Bernier case, the decision makers were clearly in Switzerland, but John Beck originally could not reach them working through Bernier's American representatives. Had he not taken the initiative to overcome this communication block with Bernier, the development effort might never have come to fruition.

The purchaser's proposal also increases the chance that it may become the basis for the subsequent work the vendor will do. By getting the proposal into the vendor's hands before supplier personnel have had a chance to work out alternative approaches on their own, the purchaser preconditions their thinking. It is certain that the supplier's people will do their own homework instead of relying on the data and figures supplied by the purchaser. In the CCC case both Bernier and the other fertilizer producer did exactly this. It is highly probable that in each case supplier personnel, as part of their homework, checked out the CCC proposal thoroughly. A complete and well-prepared proposal from the purchaser, therefore, is essential in large reverse marketing. It serves to persuade and impress not only the vendor's decision makers, but also the key people inside the purchaser's own organization.

Normally, the supply department will not have the budget, or talent, or both, to prepare such a feasibility study on its own. Thus, the supply manager is called upon to become an "idea" or project "champion" who will have to know how to enlist the appropriate internal support. For John Beck at CCC this was, obviously, a normal role he cherished and carried out well. It gained him and his department respect, credibility, and status at CCC. It was not by chance, however, that John Beck and the purchasing department achieved this high level of acceptability within CCC. Beck had worked hard at improving purchasing's contribution to CCC over many years. He had proven over time that staffing the department with high quality, well-paid personnel, looking for long-term opportunities with a major impact on the whole organization, and being in tune with corporate goals and strategies, would result in significant payoffs. For John Beck, reverse marketing was not an occasional purchasing tool to be used in case of dire need. For him it was the key procurement tool to support future corporate success.

THE MEDIUM-SIZED SUPPLIER

Thus far, supplier size has been discussed at the extreme ends, large and small. There is no sense limiting development options to these two categories, however. Clearly, medium-sized suppliers form an attractive target group. They are a logical alternative to both small and large sources, and may avoid the biggest disadvantages of either of the other categories.

Numerous examples of successful medium reverse marketing efforts exist. It is not necessary to detail any. An interesting common thread, however, of the medium suppliers studied, was the problem of supplier size-up. For a small local supplier, size-up of the organization is not difficult and can be quickly done. Similarly, for most large firms plenty of information is available and the reverse marketing effort requires a feasibility study, anyway.

Medium suppliers are a bit of a question mark. To what extent do they still exhibit small supplier behavior? Are they short of liquidity? Do they have significant technical resources? Where does their future potential lie? To what extent do they already behave like a large organization? Are they anxious or reluctant to take on new challenges? Will they really commit corporate resources to this venture or not?

Since medium suppliers may be located farther away than small suppliers, it may be more difficult to carry out a full assessment and to establish exactly what might be possible. Each vendor will have to be examined carefully for strengths and weaknesses. It is probably difficult to generalize with medium suppliers as readily as with small and large suppliers. It is this assessment task that purchasers engaged in the development of medium suppliers found difficult and challenging. They found they could be informal sometimes, and had to be highly formal in others. Sometimes they received quick answers, in others not. Sometimes the key decision maker could be easily identified, in others not.

The medium-sized supplier is probably best suited for requirements covering the bottom of the "A," all of the "B," and the top of the "C" range. (In the "ABC" classification scheme, "A" items represent 10% of the requirements in volume and 80% in dollars, "B" items, 10% of the volume and 10% of the dollars, and "C" items, 80% of the volume and 10% of the dollars.) Even the identification of which of these three classes might be most suitable in a particular case needs to be examined. Thus, the medium supplier, normally with opportunities greater than those offered by the small supplier, and smaller than those by the large supplier, forms a valuable, but challenging segment of the supplier options available.

PURCHASER SIZE

Thus far, the question of supplier size has been addressed, but this only looks at half the picture. The size of the purchaser's organization is also a factor to be considered. Until now, it has been assumed that the purchaser's organization is large enough to have at least one full-time purchasing person in its employ and at least an identifiable purchasing or supply department. This probably makes the purchaser's organization larger than the smallest supplier considered. Mathematically, there are a clear number of different match-ups when considering both purchaser and supplier size. (See Figure 7-1.) Even granting only three different sizes (small, medium, and large) for each, this creates nine possible match-ups. It would be tedious and unnecessary to discuss each. Since so far it has been assumed that the purchaser is at least of medium or large size in all of the examples considered, the case of the small purchaser needs a further look.

The Small Purchaser

The small purchaser, by definition, is in a difficult reverse marketing position. The small purchaser cannot exert economic clout like larger buyers, and probably lacks internal resources to engage in the project work necessary for large reverse marketing. The case of Mega Technologies shows that the small purchaser's position

FIGURE 7-1.
Purchaser and Supplier Size—Nine Possible Match-Ups

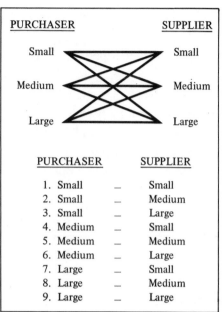

PURCHASER		SUPPLIER
1. Small	—	Small
2. Small	—	Medium
3. Small	—	Large
4. Medium	—	Small
5. Medium	—	Medium
6. Medium	—	Large
7. Large	—	Small
8. Large	—	Medium
9. Large	—	Large

is far from hopeless, however. Reverse marketing targets may be centered on smaller suppliers, which are easier to deal with. Also, provided the small purchaser can indicate that a market should exist for the product or service the small purchaser wants from a large supplier, the large supplier can do the necessary market research to check this out.

The small purchaser's best hope with large suppliers, therefore, is that other customers exist for the particular requirement at hand. Perhaps, also, the small purchaser can play the reverse public relations game, pointing out the public relations value to the larger firm if it accommodates the small purchaser's request. Clearly, however, the number of reverse marketing options open to large purchasers is considerably greater than for the small purchaser.

BRIEF SUMMARY

1. Supplier size may impact significantly on reverse marketing objectives and process.

2. Large suppliers should probably be the target when major savings are sought.

3. Small suppliers may offer attractive local options, opportunities for barter, and public relations spinoffs.

4. Large suppliers require a more extensive and formal development process.

5. Small suppliers can be developed in a more informal, quicker way.

6. Medium-sized suppliers need to be assessed carefully to establish in what ways they still behave like a small supplier, and in what ways they exhibit large supplier characteristics.

7. How supplier size affects reverse marketing objectives and the development process is shown in Figure 7–2.

FIGURE 7–2.
The Impact of Supplier Size on Reverse Marketing
Generalizations on Objectives and Process

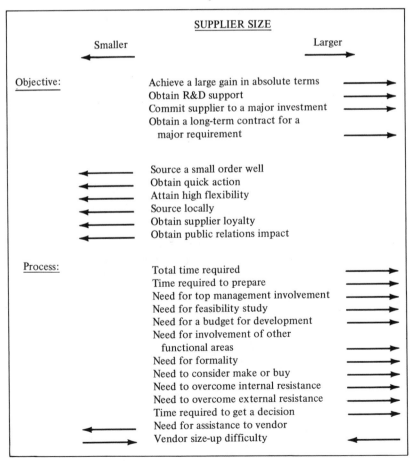

CHAPTER 8

Conclusion

THE emphasis in the foregoing chapters has been on two main themes: the potential contribution inherent in the supply function in any organization and the need for an imaginative and aggressive management stance toward supply. Neither of these ideas is particularly novel to the organizations included in this research. Certainly an aggressive top management stance towards supply translates into an aggressive approach to suppliers. Out-marketing the marketers, or reverse marketing, has substantial benefits for the organization willing to exploit new supply initiatives to the fullest. In very few of the organizations researched was the full potential of the supply area actually realized. Clair Chemical Corporation probably came the closest. The magnificent achievement of persuading a Swiss supplier to sell its recently purchased plant site, to forget about all of its engineering plans, to move to a new site and a new process, using a new material, showed reverse marketing at its finest. The total benefits to Clair Chemical exceeded $30 million per year on that deal alone. And in Clair Chemical Corporation this kind of supply initiative was not considered unusual.

To the top executive the appeal of the supply function must lie in the high payoffs from relatively low investment. And, in the case of repetitive requirements, savings may accrue from year to year. The supply area represents untapped potential difficult to duplicate elsewhere in most organizations. These days few organizations can afford to miss out on such relatively simple opportunities. Persuading vendors to join the supplier team is just as rewarding as capturing new customers.

The top management involvement will have to extend beyond

the supplier contact area. It may also be necessary to encourage supply managers to spread their wings and to adopt a more long-term and strategic perspective. Moreover, organizational obstacles may have to be removed and a favorable climate created for supply exploration. These are not, nor should they be, onerous tasks for the top executive. However, this kind of support is vital to the heavy work that needs to be done in the supply and other functional areas to dig out the opportunities and investigate their feasibility.

Reverse marketing is not limited to small suppliers, unusual source problems, and long-term contracts. Supplier size is an important factor in determining the approach and planning to be used but successful development does not depend on supplier size. The main determinant of the success or failure of reverse marketing is the purchaser. As initiator of the process he or she bears the main responsibility for implementation and results. The examples of actual organizations given in the preceding chapters indicate that the purchaser can improve the chances of success by careful planning.

The value of reverse marketing in cases of necessity is generally recognized by supply executives. Its wider scope as a contributor to organizational objectives and strategy is not as widely appreciated. Future source considerations appear to offer a host of further reverse marketing opportunities. An imaginative and aggressive approach to source creation appears to represent the ultimate in reverse marketing. Such an approach requires from the supply manager a full appreciation of the potential contributions to his or her organization. This, in turn, requires a person of top management caliber. The creation can be no better than its creator.

REVERSE MARKETING AS A PROCESS

Successful reverse marketing follows a logical sequence of steps which culminates in the realization of objectives within a required time frame. The eleven phases presented in Chapter 2 may not all be present in every reverse marketing undertaking, but an understanding of each is fundamental in order to envision the entire process in advance of making the first supplier contact. This framework for reverse marketing provides a useful checklist for purchasers as they assess their options and as they proceed with the process itself.

THE SEARCH FOR VALUE—A FUNDAMENTAL SUPPLY OBJECTIVE

The search for value is behind most supply initiatives. Value encompasses quality, quantity, delivery, price, service, and other criteria. The examples used in the preceding chapters, starting with Malston Bakery, have the common thread of striving to obtain better value for the money spent. To obtain true value, a purchaser convinces the supplier that if both parties act as a team, each will prosper. The traditional purchasing tools of value analysis/engineering, life cycle costing, purchasing research, and "best practice services" are part of the value equation, but it is the addition of reverse marketing with its long-term focus that completes the equation.

ENVIRONMENTAL, SOCIAL, AND POLITICAL CONCERNS PUT A NEW FOCUS ON REVERSE MARKETING

The notion that the purchaser might be motivated by factors other than increased value, as usually measured by price, is traditionally resisted by many practitioners. However, during the past decade, increasing attention has been paid to environmental, social, and political concerns as an impetus for reverse marketing. Heightened concern for the environment is now often taken to the point where a purchaser prefers to do business with firms that are considered "good corporate citizens." Governments initiate reverse marketing (the Plastico example) for social reasons such as assisting a depressed industry and creating jobs in a high unemployment area.

Dealing with minority suppliers, while often discouraging at first, can result in the achievement of social and altruistic objectives. Reverse marketing with small firms sharpens the business skills of purchasers by forcing them to think things through and anticipate many eventualities. As well, many of the techniques used with minority and other small suppliers can be applied to the general supply function.

In the final analysis, the dilemma in reverse marketing for environmental, social, and political reasons is one of measurability. The short, medium, and long-run benefits are more difficult to measure than those resulting from reverse marketing undertaken strictly for economic value reasons. The purchaser may not be the best person in the organization to make the final decision on the trade-offs between "softer" social concerns and "harder" economic value ones, but must identify the options and their associated costs and benefits.

NEW TECHNOLOGY INITIATIVES

Most organizations are eager to make use of new technological options, new management systems, processes, products, or services. This puts pressure on suppliers to meet this technological challenge. Reverse marketing may be vital to assure the purchaser early access to such technology.

Reverse marketing involving new technology may have a deeper motivation than simply a financial one. There may be a strong desire to be an industry leader in a new technology, as in the Mega Technologies example.

It is necessary to define well beforehand what the new technology actually will accomplish for the organization and weigh the perceived benefits against the costs and the effects on the firm as a whole. In the Mega Technologies case, Paul Hill subsequently questioned whether it had all been worth the effort, although the final outcome for Mega was certainly positive.

There may be a high risk of failure in reverse marketing with new technology and because of this the responsibilities of each party should be clearly identified at the beginning of the project. Panelectronics' Carol French saved later grief by confirming her verbal agreement with the Watson Company in letter form.

New technology-driven initiatives often require a sophisticated level of expertise, probably beyond that possessed by the supply function. However, Carol French of Panelectronics demonstrated that it was her initiative and sound basic thinking that provided the needed catalyst for the project when it seemed bogged down. New technology may offer an organization the potential to leap ahead of its competition, but its development may be complex and require a long time to come to fruition.

THE NATURE OF THE PURCHASER'S BUSINESS AND REVERSE MARKETING

Reverse marketing opportunities may be limited by the nature of the purchase requirements of an oganization. Several examples in previous chapters demonstrated that even on commodity items and other standard materials and products for which established market prices are known and regular sources do exist, reverse marketing can be used. The purchaser is not attempting to force a supplier into giving up a rightful margin of profit but rather to achieve benefits for both sides of the development. These benefits are not likely to be obvious in the case of standard materials and products, neither are they likely to arise so long as the purchaser is content to follow standard business practice. Whether in a government agency or an automobile manufacturer, the purchaser must plan to achieve reverse marketing success. The opportunities in reverse marketing may tend to be greater for those organizations whose procurement costs are a higher proportion of total revenue. Even in public and nonprofit buying, however, there may be opportunities for reverse marketing, if executives are on the alert for them.

HOW DOES A PURCHASER FIND A SOURCE TO DEVELOP?

Finding the correct source to develop is often industry or organization specific. Different industries will have different commodities, parts, or capital equipment needs that may be common to most members of a given industry. Likewise, specific organizations will have, because of unique circumstances, some area that is a likely candidate for reverse marketing. In the Malston Bakery example, emphasis on the flour ingredient was not surprising. Mega Technologies' emphasis on new equipment was equally logical.

In most cases, the selection of a source to be developed requires the same procedure as that required in any source selection. In some cases the analysis used to determine the benefits which are to accrue to both parties may point directly to one supplier only. In other cases, the choice of supplier may be wider.

The starting point in determining sources to develop should be a comprehensive look at existing suppliers. In many of the examples in the preceding chapters, it was dissatisfaction with or the complacency of existing suppliers which provided the impetus for successful reverse marketing.

In the final analysis, in determining whether any requirement is a likely candidate for reverse marketing, it is necessary to measure the gap between desirable objectives and reality; the larger the gap, the greater the need for reverse marketing.

DOES A DEVELOPED SUPPLIER RECEIVE FUTURE FAVORABLE TREATMENT BY THE PURCHASER?

Does the purchaser have an obligation—moral, actual, or potential—to the supplier as a result of reverse marketing? Would these obligations of the purchaser to the supplier not have existed had another method of source selection been employed? Will the purchaser favor one source over another because one has become a source as a result of reverse marketing and the other has not?

It is possible that a particular purchaser may have a preference for a source of his or her own creation over one from normal selection. Whether such preference is triggered by a feeling of obligation—because the supplier "tried so hard, or did so well, or lost some other business because of it"—or as an honest evaluation of the supplier's potential is the issue at hand. It is possible that the purchaser may have a soft spot for the developed supplier. This is another good reason for planning a short, medium, and long-term goal before the development is completed. There is nothing wrong and everything right about favoring an exceptional supplier over an ordinary one.

The competent procurement executive should guard against unreasonable supplier preferences on any basis. There should be no favoring of one supplier over another on the basis of how they became suppliers. The issue in the allocation of contracts and selection of suppliers is anticipated performance, a basis that should not favor a developed supplier over any other source. Nevertheless, most reverse marketing efforts require a long-term perspective, and a temporary setback should not be a reason for abandoning the whole effort.

RISK AND REVERSE MARKETING

Reverse marketing is an exercise in hope. Both the purchaser and the supplier hope that all will go smoothly and that the effort will be a success. Nevertheless, it is useful to recognize that the potential for failure is always present. Therefore, the issue as to which party is responsible for the assumption of what liability in case of failure is one that requires resolution before a deal is struck. In any case where the costs of failure are substantial, this is no minor concern. For example, the vendor may have to invest heavily in research and development, new capacity, human resources, or have to make significant supply commitments. A number of the cases described in this text involved exactly such commitment—Malston Bakery and Panelectronics are representative examples.

In a special decision-tree perspective (Figure 8–1), there are always at least two possible outcomes for any reverse marketing: success and failure. For each possible outcome—and, of course,

FIGURE 8–1.
A Simple Decision-Tree Perspective of Reverse Marketing

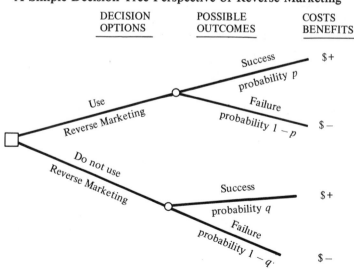

there may be a whole range of partial successes and failures in between—the risks, costs, and benefits to be borne or received by either party need to be examined. Presumably the toughest questions center on the failure cases. If failure occurs, who pays for what? The purchaser may approach this question of risk acceptance in a variety of ways (Figure 8-2).

The Conditional Approach

The conditional approach to the assumption of risk liability by the purchaser is based on one condition. If the supplier insists that the purchaser assume some or all of the risk and if the successful

FIGURE 8-2.
Three Different Approaches to Risk-sharing in Reverse Marketing

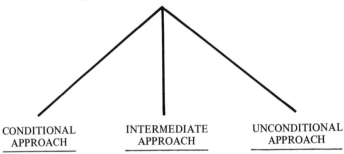

CONDITIONAL APPROACH	INTERMEDIATE APPROACH	UNCONDITIONAL APPROACH
Only if the supplier insists that the purchaser assume at least some, if not all, of the risk liability, the purchaser will negotiate. Otherwise, the risk will be totally borne by the supplier.	The supplier and purchaser jointly examine the issue of risk liability and determine what exposure is reasonable for each side as part of the whole deal.	The purchaser will predetermine to what extent the purchaser's assumption of liability in case of supplier failure will be part of the purchaser's initial and final offer, regardless of the supplier's position on this issue.

RANGE OF POSSIBLE AND (LIKELY) OUTCOMES

Purchaser assumes 0% - 100% risk.	Purchaser assumes 0% - 100% of risk.	Purchaser assumes 0% - 100% of risk.
(0% - 25%)	(20% - 70%)	(0% - 50%)

initiation of the reverse marketing effort depends on it, the purchaser is willing to make risk liability a negotiable item. The purchaser's starting position is that the supplier should be totally liable for all costs incurred in case the development efforts fail. Even though it is theoretically possible the range of outcomes could include the purchaser's full assumption of all risk, it is more likely that the deal will see a relatively minor assumption of risk by the purchaser under this approach.

The advantages of the conditional approach are fairly obvious. This agreement seems to fit the general philosophy that a purchaser should not offer a supplier something the supplier does not specifically request. The purpose of the reverse marketing effort is to achieve success. The fear of losing a significant sum in case of failure may be a good incentive to achieve success. Presumably the carrot is contained in the benefit package offered in case of success. The stick is the risk of failure. Provided the supplier is sufficiently knowledgeable, and the risk of failure not devastating, this approach offers a reasonable philosophical basis from which to start negotiating. The final outcome will be that the purchaser pays none, some, or all of the failure cost. However, the supplier has been under pressure to substantiate the reasonableness and extent of such support. Presumably, the higher the amount of risk support by the purchaser in case of failure, the lower the package price needs to be in case of success.

The Unconditional Approach

At the other end of the spectrum from the conditional approach is the unconditional approach—the purchaser unconditionally offers to underwrite all, a portion, or none of the cost of failure whether the supplier requests it or not. The unconditional approach is predetermined by the purchaser and leaves no room for negotiation or subsequent change. However, the purchaser is frank about it and raises the issue as part of the total deal and states the risk dimension unequivocally.

There may be advantages to the unconditional approach at certain times. In the first place, the unconditional unwillingness to pay any of the supplier's failure costs needs to be discussed. This is probably the most common approach used by purchasers. Please note that the same situation is achieved by the conditional route when the supplier does not request any underwriting of the risk from the purchaser. The route, however, is different; the purchaser makes this an explicit condition right from the start and both parties recognize it. The benefits package in case of success needs to be structured so as to reflect this condition. The approach Ms. French used with the Watson Company was a clear example of the unconditional approach where the purchaser was unwilling to underwrite any of the supplier's costs of failure. It should be noted, however, that in the Watson case the purchaser incurred significant testing costs on its own premises.

The remaining outcomes involving partial and full underwriting of failure costs are also possible options under the unconditional approach. By offering full or partial support up front, the purchaser shows good faith in the reverse marketing effort. It may facilitate and speed up the decision by the supplier to cooperate. The costs to the purchaser may be of lesser consequence than to the supplier. Such an approach also gives the purchaser better access to the books of the supplier and to progressive results. Thus, even in the case of failure, the insights gained, managerially and technologically, may be of benefit to further reverse marketing efforts. Presumably, the purchaser may also demand in return a better deal in the final benefits package in case of success. It is possible, for example, that in the Panelectronics case of part #503, the actual cost to Vencor of producing it was in the 25¢ to 75¢ range, while Panelectronics paid $2.50. If the development cost to Vencor was in the $100,000 range, for example, Panelectronics might have been better off offering to underwrite 50 or 100 percent of this in return for an opportunity to set the price at a 20 percent margin over actual cost. Even though at $2.50 per unit Panelectronics saved about $840,000 per year, it might have done consierably better.

There is a common purchasing reluctance to pay for something that is not actually received, and especially in the case of supplier failure to achieve hoped for results. Therefore, it is unlikely that most reverse marketing efforts using the unconditional approach would result in a purchaser's share of the risk above 50 percent.

The Intermediate Approach

The conditional and unconditional approaches to risk assumption in case of supplier failure represent two ends of a spectrum. Obviously, a large number of intermediate options exist. It is probably unwise to be overly precise about this in-between range of options;

whether they lean towards the conditional or unconditional is probably immaterial. The key characteristic of the intermediate approach is the recognition by both parties that this important issue of risk liability must be settled as part of the total deal. By raising the issue and approaching it flexibly, the purchaser may be able to strike an overall deal that makes sense for both parties.

The purchaser's assumption of risk in reverse marketing is a vital key to the whole deal. It is important to recognize that the prime purpose of the whole development is to achieve success, not failure. Therefore, the purchaser needs to structure the approach to risk so as to maximize success. No one approach is superior to another, and each case needs to be examined on its own merits.

WHY IS REVERSE MARKETING NOT USED MORE WIDELY?

If reverse marketing is such a valuable procurement tool, why is it not more widely used? The main reason for its limited use appears to be the lack of understanding of its potential by supply and other executives. So long as the purchaser is unaware of benefits that accrue from reverse marketing, there is no reason to undertake an aggressive approach to source creation. Reverse marketing is not a magic formula that solves all supply problems. It is a valuable tool when used at the right time, in the correct manner. Reverse marketing offers an exciting chance to supply managers to work cooperatively with others in the organization on opportunities and not just problems. To the imaginative and aggressive supply executive, reverse marketing is indispensable.

Reverse marketing's potential is directly related to lead time. If the requirement is urgent, no time for reverse marketing exists. Even in situations of normal lead time, there may not be enough time to do the homework and planning that reverse marketing requires. Only if extended lead time is available, or if the organization is sufficiently future oriented, can the full benefits of reverse marketing be realized (see Figure 8–3).

INTERNAL AND EXTERNAL SYNERGY

The benefits from reverse marketing stem from two sources: internal and external synergy. Internal synergy is achieved when a team approach is used to solve the supply problem at hand. The addi-

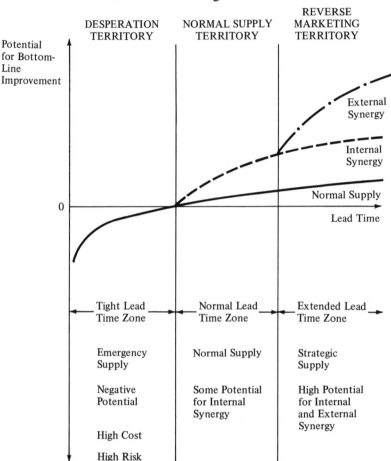

FIGURE 8–3.
Reverse Marketing's Potential

tion of marketing, operations, engineering, financial, and other inputs into the process may reveal opportunities not apparent to any single function.

External synergy comes from supplier input and involvement in the acquisition process at the appropriate times. Such supplier input may be further multiplied when lead times are extended further. Then the suppliers' suppliers can also join the team and the chain is extended.

The magnitude of the benefits will vary from situation to situation. It is difficult to claim that internal synergy will account for

50 percent of the potential and external synergy for another 50 percent. Nevertheless, it is useful to note that the potential may be massive if the full force of internal and external synergy can be unlocked. Furthermore, it is possible to have internal synergy without external synergy. However, it is difficult to have external synergy without internal synergy. One of the great benefits from reverse marketing is that it pushes the organization into internal synergy. Both reverse marketing and internal teamwork can be brought along together! Reverse marketing is not a concept that requires organization perfection before it can be implemented.

THE LONGER-TERM IMPACT
OF REVERSE MARKETING

Experience has shown that over time successful reverse marketing manages to require less lead time. As internal and external synergy builds, lead times can actually be shortened. The simple explanation is that jobs can be done faster if they are done right the first time. The end result of reverse marketing over time will change the perspective from Figure 8-3 to that of Figure 8-4. Thus, in the

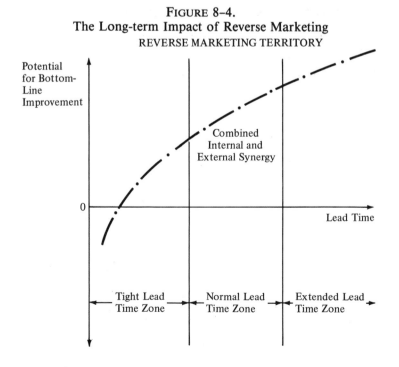

FIGURE 8-4.
The Long-term Impact of Reverse Marketing
REVERSE MARKETING TERRITORY

long term, greater supply benefits can be achieved faster as the internal and external teamwork anticipates needs and finds effective solutions faster.

The exciting aspect of reverse marketing is that it challenges the traditional view of inevitable trade-offs. Conventional wisdom used to be that good quality invariably meant a higher price. Similarly, delivery had to be taken in large quantities to get a price break. Both of these two myths have already been successfully challenged by the inventory reduction and quality forces. A parallel to both of these concepts exists in reverse marketing. In reverse marketing it is possible and reasonable to have your cake and eat it too. It is possible to set and achieve seemingly impossible objectives of high local content and good value, of superior service and an outstanding price, of great flexibility and high quality, of reliable supply and continuing price and product improvement. Traditionally, purchasers have been preconditioned by suppliers to underestimate their options. By taking the initiative and setting objectives to fit their own needs first, purchasers' chances of success increase dramatically.

Reverse marketing offers a new perspective on the scope of the potential supply contribution to organizational objectives and strategy. It is driven by the need for continuing improvement. It comes from the recognition that an aggressive and imaginative approach to suppliers is essential to a well-managed organization.

Notes

CHAPTER 1. REVERSE MARKETING

1. William H. Davidow, *Marketing High Technology* (New York: Free Press, 1986), 172.
2. Ibid., 169.
3. Ibid., 166.
4. E. Raymond Corey, *Procurement Management: Strategy, Organization, and Decision Making* (Boston: CBI Publishing, 1978), x.
5. Ibid., 2.
6. S. F. Heinritz and P. V. Farrell, *Purchasing: Principles and Applications,* 6th ed. (Englewood Cliffs, NJ: Prentice-Hall, 1981), 243.
7. D. Ammer, "Is your purchasing department a good buy?" *Harvard Business Review,* 52, No. 2 (March-April, 1974), 36–42.

CHAPTER 2. THE REVERSE MARKETING FRAMEWORK

1. Harold E. Fearon, *Purchasing Research: Concepts and Current Practice,* (New York: American Management Association, 1976).
2. Gordon L. Lippitt, *Organization Renewal: A Holistic Approach to Organization Development* (Englewood Cliffs, NJ: Prentice-Hall, 1982), 50.
3. Ibid., 54.

CHAPTER 3. VALUE AND PRICE

1. Michiel R. Leenders, Harold E. Fearon, and Wilbur B. England, *Purchasing and Materials Management,* 8th ed. (Homewood, IL: Richard D. Irwin, 1985), 112–113.

CHAPTER 4.   TECHNOLOGY
AND REVERSE MARKETING

1. R. A. More, "Developer/Adopter Relationships in New Industrial Product Situations," *Journal of Business Research,* (1986), 501–517.
2. Ibid., p. 501.

CHAPTER 5.   SOCIAL, POLITICAL,
AND ENVIRONMENTAL CONCERNS

1. Larry C. Giunipero, "Developing Effective Minority Purchasing Programs," *Sloan Management Review,* Vol. 22, No. 2, Winter 1981, pp. 33–42.
2. *The Wall Street Journal,* October 17, 1979.
3. Thomas Hout, Michael E. Quarter, and Eileen Rudden, "How Global Companies Win Out," *Harvard Business Review,* Vol. 60, No. 5 (Sept–Oct. 1982), 98–108.
4. *The Globe and Mail* (Toronto), October 26, 1981.
5. *The Globe and Mail* (Toronto), April 10, 1980, Report of Business.

CHAPTER 6.   SUPPLY TRENDS
AND REVERSE MARKETING

1. William E. Deming, *Quality, Productivity, and Competitive Position* (Cambridge: Massachusetts Institute of Technology, Center for Advanced Engineering Study, 1984).
2. Philip B. Crosby, *Quality Is Free* (New York: McGraw-Hill, 1979).
3. Michiel R. Leenders, Harold E. Fearon, and Wilbur B. England, *Purchasing and Materials Management,* 8th ed. (Homewood, IL: Richard D. Irwin, 1985), 123–124.
4. Richard J. Schonberger and James P. Gilbert, "Just-in-Time Purchasing: A Challenge for U.S. Industry," *California Management Review,* Vol. 26, No. 1 (Fall 1983), 54–68.
5. Deming, *Quality, Productivity, and Competitive Position.*
6. David H. Farmer, "Source Decision-Making in the Multi-National Company Environment," *Journal of Purchasing and Materials Management,* Vol. 8 (February 1972), 5–17, at pp. 9 and 10. Reprinted with permission from the National Association of Purchasing Management, Inc.
7. Ibid., at pp. 16 and 17.

Index